To my friend Shay on your
7th birthday
James Joyce

EVERYTHING YOU NEED TO KNOW ABOUT SCIENCE

First published 2009 by Kingfisher
This edition published 2011 by Kingfisher
an imprint of Macmillan Children's Books
a division of Macmillan Publishers Limited
20 New Wharf Road, London N1 9RR
Basingstoke and Oxford
Associated companies around the world
www.panmacmillan.com

3 5 7 9 8 6 4 2

2TR/0612/WKT/SCHOY/140MA

ISBN 978-0-7534-3400-0

Produced in association with the Science Museum
www.sciencemuseum.org.uk
Consultant: Dan Albert

NOTE TO READERS
The website addresses listed in this book are correct at the time of going to print.
However, due to the ever-changing nature of the internet, website addresses and
content can change. Websites can contain links that are unsuitable for children.
The publisher cannot be held responsible for changes in website addresses or
content, or for information obtained through third-party websites. We strongly
advise that internet searches should be supervised by an adult.

EVERYTHING YOU NEED TO KNOW ABOUT SCIENCE

Dr Mike Goldsmith

KINGFISHER

Contents

Living things

Space

Using this book

As well as lots of information, this book has many special ideas in it to help you enjoy it more. There are superscience features and amazing facts to astound, vocabulary notepads to expand your word sense, difficult questions with fascinating answers, and great activities and games. Enjoy exploring!

▶ Fact box

Look out for the exclamation mark on these boxes. Each fact box contains amazing facts about the subject matter that is being described. This fact box is from the chapter called 'Numbers and shapes'. You will find it on page 22.

Egg shapes

Some seabirds that nest on cliffs lay eggs that have one end that is much more pointed than the other, unlike other birds' eggs. This shape means that the eggs roll in circles when they are moved or knocked, and do not fall off the cliff ledge.

Superscience

Inside the Earth

If you could look inside the Earth, you would see that the soil and oceans are a very thin layer on top of a rocky crust. Beneath this is a 'mantle' of different rocks. Under that is a layer of hot, liquid metal. The Earth's inner core is made of very hot, solid metal.

◀ Superscience box

You can find out in-depth information about exciting science. Look out for the zig-zag electricity. This superscience feature is from the chapter called 'Space'. You will find it on page 136.

VOCABULARY

engine
A machine that uses fuel to make things move.

compound
A combination of two or more things.

rotor
A rotating part of a machine.

◄ Vocabulary notepad

There are sometimes difficult words used in the text that need further explaining, so there is a notepad specially for this task. This vocabulary notepad is from the chapter called 'How the world works'. You will find it on page 49.

► Question circle

Everyone has questions they are dying to ask. You will find circles with questions and their answers in every chapter. This question circle is from the chapter called 'The world of materials'. You will find it on page 88.

IS BURNING FUEL A PROBLEM?

The oil, coal and gas that we burn makes the world warmer and dirtier. So we also make power in other ways – from falling water, waves, sunlight, wind and from splitting atoms too.

► Can you find?

These features will test what you can spot and name in the pictures. This flower-shaped Can you find? is from the chapter called 'Living things'. You will find it on page 98.

CAN YOU FIND?

1. leaves
2. two tongues
3. wings
4. roots
5. beaks
6. lily pads

▶ Creative corner

The splodge of paint says it all! This is where you can let your creative self run wild. The book is packed with great things to make and do. This creative corner is from the chapter called 'Space'. You will find it on page 133.

▼ At the bottom of every right-hand page in the book you will find one or two useful websites. These have been carefully chosen to add to the information on the page.

CREATIVE CORNER

Walk through the Solar System

In a park, stick a flag in the ground. This is the Sun. Take three paces and stick in a flag for Mercury. Now put flags down after these distances:

3 paces (Venus)

2 (Earth)

4 (Mars)

28 (Jupiter)

34 (Saturn)

75 (Uranus)

84 (Neptune)

▲ You will need

Plain and coloured paper, card, glue, string, scissors, pencils, modelling clay, crayons, paints, paint brushes, drinking straws, plastic cups, bowls and plates, glass bottles, wool, sticky tape, balloons, wooden rods, magnifying glass, cotton buds, compass, funnel, chalk, table-tennis ball, sweet wrappers, torches, postcard, food colouring, wooden spoon.

Numbers and shapes

Without numbers, our lives would be very different – there would be no science, no money and no computers. And to make buildings, machines, clothes and almost anything else, people need to understand shapes. We can do very complicated things, such as flying to the Moon, using the science of numbers and shapes.

Numbers

In mathematics, we can work with numbers using 'operations' such as adding, subtracting, multiplying and dividing. All the sciences rely on mathematics.

▶ It is hard to imagine a world without numbers. We use them to tell the time, buy things, catch buses and choose TV channels. And we could not do any science without them.

WHAT IS THE LARGEST NUMBER?
There is no largest number. However big a number is, we can always make it bigger by adding another number to it.

Arabic	0	1	2	3	4	5	6	7	8	9	10
Roman		I	II	III	IV	V	VI	VII	VIII	IX	X
Chinese	〇	一	二	三	四	五	六	七	八	九	十
Binary	0000	0001	0010	0011	0100	0101	0110	0111	1000	1001	1010

▲ The way people write down numbers has changed through history. Zero was invented more recently than the other numbers. Binary numbers are used by computers.

How many numbers can you see on this page? And which is the largest?

Nature's numbers

1, 3 and 5 are examples of what we call 'odd' numbers, and 2, 4 and 6 are examples of 'even' numbers. Almost every animal on Earth has an even number of legs. Most flowers have an odd number of petals. If you pick a flower, there is a good chance it has 5 petals – but no one is sure why!

Superscience

Negative numbers

Numbers less than zero are called 'negative' numbers. For example, 2 minus 5 gives the negative number –3 ('minus three'). Negative numbers are used for low temperatures. A freezer is about –18°C, 18 degrees colder than freezing water.

-7 -6 -5 -4 -3 -2 -1 **0** 1 2 3 4 5 6 7

Using numbers

In mathematics, we can work with numbers using 'operations' such as adding, subtracting, multiplying and dividing. All the sciences rely on these mathematical operations.

WHY DO WE COUNT TO TEN? ❓
Our number system is based on a system of 10 digits from 0 to 9. It is an easy system to learn because we can count on our 10 fingers – or our 10 toes!

▲ Adding means putting numbers together. Sometimes we use counting to add things. For example, putting 2 nuts with another 2 and counting how many you have gives 4, which we write as 2 + 2 = 4. How many nuts will the squirrel have if he adds one more?

▲ Subtracting means taking a number away from another number. If you have 5 strawberries and eat 3, you have 2 left. We can write this as 5 − 3 = 2. We call things like '5 − 3 = 2' or '1 + 1 = 2' sums, or calculations.

▲ Multiplying is like adding over and over again. If 4 children each have 3 sweets, we can work out that there are 12 sweets by adding: 3 + 3 + 3 + 3 = 12. Or we can do it by multiplying: 3 x 4 = 12.

▲ Dividing is like sharing things out. If 9 cards are divided equally between 3 people, then each person will get 3 cards. We can write this as 9 ÷ 3 = 3.

CREATIVE CORNER

Secret codes

Write down the letters of the alphabet, and number them from 1 to 26. Write a message, and label its letters with their numbers. Copy the numbers onto a new piece of paper. Only your friends will understand the message – if you tell them the secret!

INTERNET LINKS: www.woodlands-junior.kent.sch.uk/maths/interactive/

Fractions

When we divide something, the bits we end up with are called fractions. If you share a banana with a friend, you each get a fraction of the banana. If you share it equally, the fraction is $1/2$ ('one-half').

▶ These three slices are different fractions of a cake. If you cut the biggest slice in half, the two new slices would each be one-quarter of the cake. We can write this as a sum: $1/2 \times 1/2 = 1/4$.

WHAT DOES PER CENT MEAN?

Cent means 100, and a 'century' is 100 years. 'Per cent' means 'hundredth', so 5% (five per cent) is 5 hundredths, or $5/100$.

1/6 (one-sixth)

1/3 (one-third)

a quarter

one-fourth

2/8

0.25

25%

4/16

1/4

two-eighths

▲ The broken-off piece of chocolate is a fraction of the whole bar. The same fraction can be written in many ways. All of the numbers above are different ways of saying the same thing! The figure 0.25 (nought-point-two-five) is called a decimal. Can you write $1/2$ as a decimal?

$1/2$ (one-half)

Endless fractions

Sometimes when we write a fraction as a decimal, the answer is short and simple: $1/10$ (one-tenth) becomes 0.1. But if we write $1/3$ as a decimal, we get 0.3333… the threes go on forever! As an example, you could find $1/9$ (one-ninth) as a decimal by typing $1 \div 9 =$ into a calculator.

CREATIVE CORNER

Fractions and shapes

Fold a square piece of paper in half and in half again. Now fold the paper diagonally. Cut a spike out of the paper, then unfold it. Your star has eight points, and the shape you cut is one-eighth of the star.

Measuring

We measure all sorts of things, such as weight or length. Each type of measurement has its own unit. Some have several units: metres and kilometres are both units of length.

▲ Machines are often used to measure things. This machine is used to weigh ingredients for cooking.

150cm

120cm

90cm

60cm

30cm

◄ We sometimes use a chart to measure height. This chart shows that the girl is 120cm tall (which is the same as 1.2m). How high is she able to reach?

CAN YOU FIND?

Which boat:

1. Is shortest?
2. Is biggest?
3. Has a tall mast?
4. Is the fastest?

Superscience

Choosing units

Scientists use different units for things of different sizes. The sizes of atoms are measured in angstroms. There are 100 million angstroms in one centimetre. Distances to stars are measured in light-years, with 9 million million kilometres in one light-year.

Tugboat

Accuracy

Scientists can use atomic clocks to measure time to as tiny a measure as a trillionth of a second. We call measurements like this 'accurate'. When we do not need accuracy, we 'round' the answer up or down. Someone who is 140.12cm tall will round their height down to 140cm.

▶ Volume is the amount of space that something fills up. We can measure the volume of milk (or any other liquid) by pouring it into a measuring jug. The jug's scale may be marked in litres or pints: these are two different units of volume.

Scale

▼ Sometimes we do not need exact measurements. Instead, we can get a rough answer by estimating. Try estimating the height of the yacht in this picture in centimetres. Now measure the height with a ruler to see how close your estimate is.

Tall ship

Cruiser

Speedboat

Yacht

Rowing boat

Canoe

INTERNET LINKS: http://pbskids.org/clifford/games/measuring_up.html

Charts and graphs

Numbers are often easier to understand if they are shown as pictures. Charts and graphs are both types of number-picture. Colours, shapes and labels can make the pictures more useful.

▼ Bar charts are good for seeing the numbers of different things. From this one, can you see how many ladybirds there are in the garden?

| Ladybird | Beetle | Bee | Butterfly | Snail |

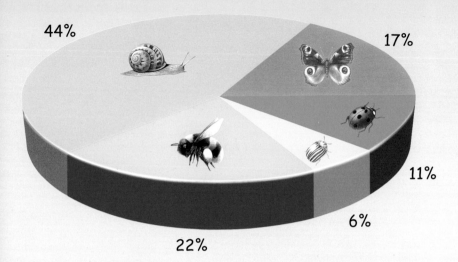

44%

17%

11%

6%

22%

◄ Pie charts can show how a group of things, such as the animals in this garden, is split up into different types. The bigger the slice, the more there are of that type of animal. For example, here 44% of the animals are snails.

► Graphs can show how things change over time. This one shows the height of a growing sunflower on different days of a week. It was 225cm tall on Monday. Four days later, it was 245cm tall. What day was that?

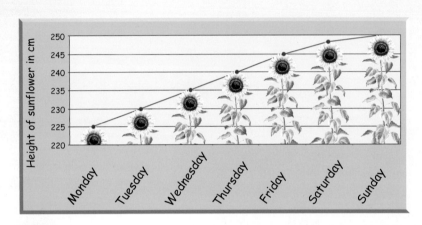

Height of sunflower in cm

250
245
240
235
230
225
220

Monday Tuesday Wednesday Thursday Friday Saturday Sunday

CREATIVE CORNER

Maths map

Maps are another type of scientific picture. In the middle of a big piece of paper, draw a small picture of the room you are in, as if you are looking down on it. Include some of the furniture, and add some labels. Leave gaps for doors and windows. Now add the next-door rooms to make a map of your house.

INTERNET LINKS: http://pbskids.org/cyberchase/math-games/bugs-in-the-system

Shapes and angles

Many things made by people have simple 'regular' shapes. Some natural things are regular too, such as the round pupils of your eyes. But many natural things are complicated and 'irregular' in shape, like trees. The science of shapes is called geometry.

▲ Oblongs are also called rectangles. If the sides of a rectangle are all the same length, it is called a square. CDs are round – but CD boxes are square.

Pythagoras (c.560–480BCE)
Pythagoras related numbers to sounds. He showed that if a string on a musical instrument was played at the same time as a string half its length they would sound good together.

◄ Circles are very useful – imagine a bike with wheels of any other shape! The width of a circle is called its 'diameter', and the length around it is called its 'circumference'.

Superscience

Endless number

The length of the outer edge of a circle can be worked out by multiplying its width by about 3.14. This number is called 'pi' (symbol π). Pi cannot be written down exactly, because it goes on forever!

▲ Bees use hexagons (shapes with six equal sides) to build their hives. This shape gives the bees the most storage space while using the smallest amount of building material.

▲ A triangle is a strong shape, so it is sometimes used for building. Try making a triangle by pinning together 3 drinking straws, and a square from 4 straws. See which is stronger.

▶ Angles are used to label the steepness of slopes. The larger the number, the steeper the slope. A 90° (90 degree) angle is called a 'right angle'. What angles can you measure in the mountains in this picture?

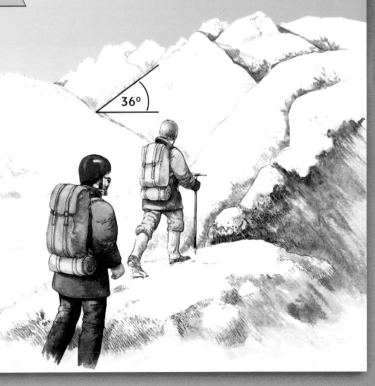

Solid shapes

Flat shapes such as squares and circles are 'two-dimensional' – each flat shape has a height and a width. Solid shapes such as cubes, spheres and people, are 'three-dimensional'. They have a depth as well as a height and width.

▼ Bricks and shoe boxes are cuboid in shape. Cubes and cuboids are good for building, because they fit together without leaving gaps. Grains of salt are tiny natural cubes. Some natural things, such as bubbles and planets, are spheres. We store things in cylinders, but they can also be used to move heavy things.

Euclid (c.330–260BCE)
Euclid wrote a set of books on geometry which have been used ever since. In them, he showed how to work out many things about shapes.

Egg shapes
Some seabirds that nest on cliffs lay eggs that have one end that is much more pointed than the other, unlike other birds' eggs. This shape means that the eggs roll in circles when they are moved or knocked, and do not fall off the cliff ledge.

Cube-shaped stone blocks were moved on cylindrical rollers.

This pyramid is made up of cubes and cuboids. Every pyramid has four triangular sides and a square base.

The Sun is a sphere.

CREATIVE CORNER

Symmetry

Put a blob of paint in the middle of a piece of paper. Fold the paper in half, then open it. The pattern you have made is symmetrical – the left half is exactly the same as the right half. Any shape that can be cut into two identical halves is symmetrical.

INTERNET LINKS: www.bgfl.org/bgfl/custom/resources_ftp/client_ftp/ks2/maths/3d/index.htm

Time

Days and years are natural time-units. The Earth spins once a day, and goes round the Sun once a year. Long ago, people invented hours, minutes and seconds to help them tell the time.

▼ Lightning lasts less than one second. When things happen in such a short time we cannot see them properly. Try watching a soap bubble as it bursts!

Superscience

Natural clocks

We have natural clocks inside us. These 'biological clocks' or 'body clocks' tell us when it is time to sleep. They allow us to 'feel' whether things – such as journeys - are lasting for a few minutes or several hours.

▶ We sometimes measure long periods of time in centuries. This tree is centuries old. It was a seed long before many of your great–great–grandparents were born.

Hours

23:55 oo

Minutes | Seconds

▲ We use clocks and watches to tell the time. Clocks with hands are called 'analogue' clocks. Clocks with numbers are called 'digital' clocks. This one is both! The same time can be written in several ways, for example '11.55pm', '23:55' and 'five to twelve'.

CREATIVE CORNER

Shadow clocks

On a sunny morning, use a lump of modelling clay to fix a stick upright in the ground. Every hour, mark its shadow with chalk and label the time. The next sunny day, your marks will tell you the time. The first clocks worked like this.

Computers

Computers are all around us. They are complicated machines that work with numbers and information. They follow sets of instructions (programs or software). Computers use binary numbers to do sums (see page 11).

Viruses

When you get ill, you may have caught a germ called a virus. Viruses of a different sort can affect computers, and make them go wrong. There are more than a million computer viruses and hundreds of new ones appear every day. Computers use special software as protection from these viruses.

◄ Cars are designed using calculations and drawings. This used to be done on paper, but it is much easier to use a computer. The shape of this car can be changed at the press of a button.

Superscience

Artificial Intelligence

'Artificially Intelligent' computers behave as if they can think. Some understand spoken questions and answer them. Others land planes, recognize people or direct traffic. Many people think that, in 50 years, some computers will be cleverer than humans.

▲ The first computers were built in the 1940s and filled whole rooms. They could do less than microchips like this one. Microchips are the 'thinking' parts of computers.

▶ This is a computer generated image. As well as looking realistic it can also move like a real animal. Many movies use computer generated images (CGI).

▶ Computers help us keep track. This display gives information about planes landing and taking off from an airport. The air-traffic controller uses the information to make sure the planes keep at safe distances from each other.

INTERNET LINKS: http://library.thinkquest.org/5862/

Robots

A robot is a moving machine that does complicated tasks. Most robots are controlled by computers. They follow instructions, but also do some things for themselves. Some robot lawnmowers plug themselves in to recharge after mowing grass.

WHICH WAS THE FIRST ROBOT?
Lifelike mechanical animals and people called 'automata' were built in the 18th century, but the first modern robot appeared in 1961. It was a factory robot called UNIMATE.

◀ This robot, called ASIMO, moves like a human being, and can recognize faces and sounds. It can also climb stairs. Not many robots are built to look like people. Instead, their bodies are designed for the jobs they do.

Superscience

Tomorrow's robots
Robots are being improved in many ways. They may soon be able to change their shapes, mend themselves when they go wrong and become much cleverer. In future, there will be many robot cleaners, security guards, soldiers, nurses and fire-fighters.

► Every space shuttle had a robot arm. The arm could be used to launch and catch satellites, and helped to build the ISS (see page 151). The camera on the arm meant that it could be used by the astronauts to check the shuttle for damage.

Arm

Space robots
Robots have explored many more worlds than human space-travellers (see page 152). They have been to every planet in the Solar System. Robots can cope with heat, cold, sudden changes of speed and long-lasting journeys better than any astronaut can. Also, their spaceships are simpler because, unlike astronauts, there is no need for robots to return to Earth.

▲ Dante is a robot built to collect samples from volcanoes for scientists to study. Robots are often used in dangerous places like this. An earlier version of Dante actually fell into a volcano!

► Nearly all of today's robots work in factories. They do jobs that are too dangerous or boring for people. Many cars are built almost entirely by robots, like the ones on this production line.

INTERNET LINKS: www.thetech.org/exhibits/online/robotics/index.html

The internet

The internet is a worldwide system of computers, all connected to each other. Using one computer, you can see words and pictures from many millions of others. And you can send and receive messages too.

HOW MANY WEBSITES ARE THERE?

There are over a billion websites. However, no one knows the exact number and there are more every day.

A website is a collection of words and pictures that you can see when you use the internet. Some websites include sounds and videos.

Superscience

Virtual reality

The internet lets you play adventure games with other people. In a virtual reality system, you can see and hear the game all around you, and interact with it. You need special equipment and computers to do this.

This boy is wearing a special virtual reality headset that shows dinosaurs all around him.

Emails are messages that are typed and then sent to other people over the internet.

Tim Berners-Lee (born 1955)
The internet developed over many years, as more computers were 'networked' (linked up). Berners-Lee worked out a method for them to communicate with each other. He used this method for the first time in 1990, which created the world wide web (www).

With the right equipment, you can speak to people over the internet. You can see them and be seen by them.

▲ The internet is made of many millions of computers. They keep in touch with each other by using phone lines and radio signals. All the things you can see on the internet make up what is called the world wide web (often just called the web).

INTERNET LINKS: www.woodlands-junior.kent.sch.uk/besmart/cool2.html

Now you know!

▲ We measure things in many ways and for many reasons. Machines can make very accurate measurements.

▲ To work with numbers, we use 'operations' such as addition, subtraction, multiplication and division.

▲ People all over the world use numbers to help them do all sorts of things.

▶ Different shapes have different uses. For instance, wheels work well because they are circles.

▲ We can make pictures called charts and graphs from measurements and numbers.

| 0000 | 0001 | 0010 | 0011 | 0100 | 0101 | 0110 | 0111 | 1000 | 1001 | 1010 |

▲ Computers use binary numbers, which are written using only 1s and 0s.

▼ Many of the world's computers are linked together to form the Internet.

◀ Robots are computer-controlled machines that move. Many robots work in factories.

How the world works

The world is a very complicated place, but it is controlled by simple laws. This chapter tells you about these laws, almost all of which were only discovered during the last few centuries. Using the laws, scientists have shown that things which seem very different, such as sound and light, or electricity and magnetism, are closely linked.

Colour

Light behaves like tiny waves, a bit like ripples on a pond, and different colours are like different sorts of ripple. Red light is made of long waves, and blue light waves are shorter.

▶ White light is a mixture of all the colours. We can see this when there is a rainbow – the Sun's white light is split up into the many colours that make it up. Black is not really a colour. It is the absence of any colour!

Kelly green

Pink

Crimson

Superscience

Invisible colours

Waves that are shorter than those of violet light (ultraviolet) are invisible. However, they affect us by giving us a sun tan or sunburn. Waves that are longer than those of red light (infrared) are also invisible. We can feel these as heat, for example from the Sun.

Tangerine

People can see more than a million different colours. Only a few hundred of these have been given names, including those shown below.

Brown

Golden yellow

Ultramarine

Cyan   Yellow

Magenta

◄ All colours can be mixed from four tubes of paint: white, and the three primary colours magenta, cyan and yellow. Cyan mixed with yellow, for example, will give green. The final colour depends on how much of each tube is used.

CREATIVE CORNER

Mixing coloured lights

Find some red, blue and green sweet wrappers that you can see through. Tape them over the ends of three small torches. In a dark room, shine two or three torches together on a piece of white paper. The coloured lights mix together in a different way from the coloured paints (above).

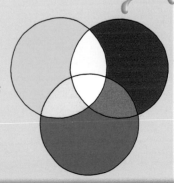

Light and dark

During the daytime, we can see the world around us because it is full of light from the Sun. At night, we use electric light, candles or moonlight. Without light, it is completely dark, so we cannot see anything.

SPEED OF LIGHT
Light travels at an incredible speed – about 300,000km a second. This is three million times faster than a racing car. It is fast enough to go around the world in less than one second.

▲ Candles (above left) were invented about 5,000 years ago, and they burn wax to make light. Light bulbs (above right) were invented in 1879 and give much brighter light. They use electricity to make a wire or a gas glow.

◄ A mirror is a piece of smooth, polished glass or metal. You can see yourself in it because the light from you bounces straight back from the mirror. This is called reflection. Light will bounce off most objects, but it usually scatters in all directions.

▲ Lenses are made of clear plastic or glass, and have special shapes so that light bends when it passes through them. Lenses can be used to make things look larger.

◄ 'Nocturnal' animals sleep during the day, and are active at night. This African bushbaby has huge eyes. This is so that it can see when there is very little light.

CREATIVE CORNER

Making coloured shadows

Tape a clear red sweet paper over one torch and a clear green paper over another. In a dark room, put the torches on the floor, far apart but both pointing at the same part of a white wall. Stand between the torches and the wall. You will have two coloured shadows!

Sound

When a whistle is blown, the air around it is squashed many times each second. The series of squashes is called a sound wave. The sound wave travels through the air to our ears.

▲ When a lion roars, the air is squashed very hard so we hear a loud sound. A kitten's small lungs can only squash the air a little, so it makes a quieter sound.

? CAN YOU HEAR MORE THAN YOUR PARENTS?
You can hear some sounds that your parents cannot hear at all. As people get older, their ears get worse at hearing high-pitched sounds.

2. Sound waves travel through the air.

1. A girl talks to her friend.

▲ Sound travels through solid objects and water as well as through the air. If your ears are under the water and someone taps on the bath, the sound goes through the bath and the water, and you can hear it.

▲ The girl is singing as loudly as the man, but she does not sound the same. The main difference is that the sounds she makes are higher in pitch. In high-pitched sounds, the squashes are close together.

▶ When the girl (left) speaks, folds of skin in her throat wobble to make sound waves. Some of the waves reach the ears of this boy.

3. Sound waves travel down the ear canal to the ear drum.

4. The ear makes tiny electrical signals when it receives sounds.

5. The signals are sent to the brain.

INTERNET LINKS: www.bbc.co.uk/schools/scienceclips/ages/5_6/sound_hearing.shtml

Music and noise

Noise is sound that we do not want to hear. It is often made up of complicated sound waves of many different lengths, all jumbled together. Music has simpler sound waves. It is usually 'harmonious', which means the pitches of the different sounds that make it up fit together well.

?

WHEN WAS MUSIC INVENTED
The oldest known musical instrument is a 50,000-year-old flute. Such flutes were played by Neanderthals, prehistoric relatives of human beings.

◀ Sounds are made by something vibrating (wobbling). A drum's skin vibrates when it is struck by a drumstick. This makes the air around the drum vibrate too, and those vibrations carry the sound to our ears.

Microphone　　　Speaker

Amplifier　　Sound waves

▲ Planes can be very noisy, particularly when flying close overhead. If noise is loud enough, it can cause damage to our hearing.

▲ A microphone changes sound waves into patterns of electricity. An amplifier makes the patterns stronger, and a loudspeaker changes them back into sound waves again so we can hear them.

CREATIVE CORNER

Make a xylophone

Take six glass bottles and put a different amount of water in each one. Play tunes on the bottles with a wooden spoon. The fuller bottles have more mass, which wobbles more slowly. This means that the fuller bottles produce a lower-pitched sound.

▲ This marching band has all kinds of brass instruments, including horns, trumpets and a tuba. Blowing into brass instruments sets the air inside them vibrating. This makes the sounds we hear.

INTERNET LINKS: www.creatingmusic.com/

Hot and cold

The hotter something is, the faster the molecules in it move. Heat always spreads out. If you touch a hot object, some heat spreads to you and the molecules (see page 72) in your skin move faster. Skin contains receptors that allow us to feel heat and cold.

▲ Temperature is a measure of how hot something is. Our bodies work properly only if they are at the right temperature. On hot days we keep our bodies from overheating by drinking plenty of water, sweating and staying in the shade.

Superscience

Absolute zero

When the molecules in an object stop moving, the object can get no colder. This is because it has no more heat to lose. The temperature at which this happens is 273.15 degrees below the temperature at which water turns to ice. This is written as $-273.15°C$. This temperature is called absolute zero.

◄ Cold is a lack of heat. Heat spreads out from objects until they have cooled to the same temperature as their surroundings. The fur coat of this panda is an insulator, slowing down the spread of heat from its body.

► Heat always moves from a hot object to a cool one. How fast it does this depends on how different the objects are in temperature and how easily the heat can flow. Insulators, such as fur, are more difficult for heat to move through than conductors, such as metal.

Heat moves easily through some solid materials by conduction. Conduction makes the handle of the kettle hot.

Heat is transferred by convection when hot gas (the flames) or liquid (the water) move around.

WHERE IS THE COLDEST PLACE ON EARTH?
Temperatures as low as −89°C have been measured in Antarctica. It is a part of the Earth that turns only slightly towards the Sun.

Heat can transfer through air or space by radiation. People nearby would feel the radiated heat from this camp fire.

CREATIVE CORNER

Make a thermometer
Half-fill a clear glass bottle (about 500ml) with cold water. Add some food colouring. Put a clear drinking straw in the bottle. Now seal the bottle with modelling clay. Make sure the straw does not touch the bottom of the bottle. The water will travel up the straw if you put your thermometer in warm water. Thermometers like this work because the liquids in them get bigger when they get hotter.

Pushes and pulls

Scientists call pushes and pulls 'forces'. Things do not need to touch to push or pull each other. Massive objects such as the Earth pull strongly on other objects. This is called the force of gravity.

▼ The Earth's gravity pulls more on two people than on one. If two people sit at one end of a seesaw, it will be pulled down harder than the end with only one person on it.

▲ If a force is spread over a big area, it does not press hard – the 'pressure' is low. A hammer cannot sink into wood, but a hammered nail can. Its small point means the force is only spread over a small area, so the pressure on the wood is high.

◄ If you let go of a spinning roundabout, you would be thrown off. The roundabout is forcing you round in a circle, while your body tends to move in a straight line.

▲ The Earth's gravity is not felt by astronauts when they are in orbit. They have the same mass (the amount of stuff they are made of) as on Earth, but no weight.

Isaac Newton (1643–1727)

Isaac Newton discovered the laws that tell us how things move. He worked out how the strength of gravity affects different objects in different places. He also made discoveries about light and mathematics.

▲ No matter how heavy a person is, or how widely they swing, the swing takes roughly the same time to move backwards and forwards.

CREATIVE CORNER

Experiment with air pressure

Put a postcard on top of a glass full of water. Now turn over the glass while holding the card. Take your hand away and the card will stay in place. The air constantly presses on everything. This air pressure holds the card in place.

Motion

Everything is in motion. Even when you stand still, you are moving with the Earth as it travels through space. To start something moving, it needs to be pushed or pulled. Then, it will keep moving without any more pushing, unless something slows it down.

▼ The speed of a car is how far it goes in a particular time. If it keeps going at 100km/h for 1 hour, it will go 100km. Its streamlined shape and smooth surface mean that air slips past easily and does not slow it down much.

Galileo (1564–1642)
Galileo worked in many areas of science. He explained the way objects move, fall and swing, He also used a telescope (see p.146) to study the Moon and the planets.

WHICH IS THE FASTEST ANIMAL?

The peregrine falcon can dive at 320km/h. The fastest land animal is the cheetah, which can run at 110km/h. The fastest human can only reach 37km/h.

▲ Moving things are slowed down by the air and the ground. Skis and hard snow are both smooth, so this skier can keep moving fast without having to push too hard.

▶ When a lift starts going up, you feel yourself being pressed down to the floor. This is because the lift is speeding up, or accelerating.

▲ Rough and rubbery surfaces slow things down easily. We say they have more 'friction'. Brakes have a lot of friction, and can slow down and stop a bike wheel.

CREATIVE CORNER

Tabletop experiment

Put a tablecloth on a small table and lay it with plastic plates, bowls and cups. Hold two corners of the tablecloth firmly at arms' length. Now pull it off the table, hard and fast. The things on the table should stay where they are! We say that this is due to the objects' 'inertia'.

Machines

A machine is something that helps people to do work. Sometimes a machine is powered by an engine. For example, the wheels and axles of a car are machines that are turned by the car's engine.

▲ A screwdriver is a lever: the handle turns in a big circle and the shaft turns in a smaller circle. This twists the screw more strongly than a hand could.

Superscience

Nanotechnology

It is possible to build tiny machines out of atoms and molecules (see p.66). So far, these machines have been very simple, but one day it may be possible to build tiny robots from them.

Rope

Wheel

▶ This is a compound pulley, in which a rope is passed over four wheels. The man can lift a weight four times heavier than he could on his own.

Archimedes (c.287–212BCE)

Archimedes was a scientist who built many machines to defend his city from attack. It is said that he used mirrors to reflect sunlight onto ships to set them on fire. He probably invented the compound pulley.

Rotor

VOCABULARY

engine
A machine that uses fuel
to make things move.

compound
A combination of two
or more things.

rotor
A rotating part of
a machine.

▶ The world is full of
complicated machines,
such as helicopters. All of them
are built up from many simple
machines. For instance, the rotors
of this helicopter are combinations
of wheels and wedges.

▶ On this building site, one person
uses a rod as a lever to move
a heavy stone. Another hits
a wedge with a mallet.
The wedge splits stones
because it pushes
sideways harder
than the mallet
presses it down.
The wheelbarrow
combines a lever
and wheels.

Lever

Lever

Wedge

Wheel

INTERNET LINKS: www.mikids.com/Smachines.htm

Floating and flying

When a boat is launched, it pushes aside a certain amount of water. It floats because it weighs less than this water. In the same way, a balloon flies because it weighs less than the air.

WHEN WAS THE FIRST SUBMARINE BUILT

There are 2,000-year-old legends about submarines. The earliest submarine we know of was built in 1605. It sank, but one built in 1620 worked.

▲ Planes are heavier than air, but they can fly because their engines keep them moving. Their wings are shaped so that they are pushed upwards by the air they fly through.

▶ A boat is built of parts that are mostly heavier than water. But boats are hollow, and filled with air. This means that the whole boat weighs less than the same amount of water. This is why it floats.

Superscience

Supersonic flight

Supersonic planes can fly faster than the speed of sound. The speed of sound is roughly 1,200km/h, although it is faster at higher temperatures. When a plane flies faster than the speed of sound, it makes a very loud booming noise.

Nylon envelope

Hot air rising

Propane burner

Gondola to carry passengers

▶ This balloon floats because it is filled with hot air, which is lighter than the cooler air around it. Toy balloons float because they are filled with a gas called helium, which is lighter than air.

CREATIVE CORNER

Moving air

Put a table-tennis ball into a funnel. Now hold it above your head and blow into the small end. Keep blowing while you turn the funnel sideways. The ball will stay in the funnel. An effect like this provides the 'lift' that makes a plane fly.

INTERNET LINKS: www.nasa.gov/audience/forstudents/k-4/stories/ames-how-planes-fly-slideshow.html

Electricity

Electricity is part of all our lives. Most homes are full of electrical equipment, and hardly anything can be made without it. We can actually see electricity when it flashes across the sky as lightning.

▼ Homes are supplied with 'mains' electricity, which comes from power stations (see pp.58–59). When something does not conduct electricity easily, it heats up, and may glow with light. This is how toasters and electric cookers work. Things that do not conduct electricity are called insulators.

Bulb — Battery

▲ Electricity flows along conductors, such as these wires. They are connected to a bulb and battery to make a 'circuit'. Electricity flows round it, lighting the bulb.

Telephone

Fridge freezer

Microwave

Blender

Toaster

Dishwasher

Washing machine

CAN YOU FIND?
1. a dial
2. an aerial
3. control buttons
4. a digital display
5. electric machines
6. a wire

James Clerk Maxwell (1831–1879)

Before Maxwell, many facts were known about electricity and magnetism, but he was able to pull them all together. He predicted that radio waves existed, and made many other scientific discoveries.

► Some electrical equipment is powered by batteries. Some batteries can no longer be used when their power is exhausted. The ones in this laptop can be recharged by plugging into the mains.

▲ In a dark room, you can sometimes see sparks of light when you take off your pullover. You may also hear crackling sounds. Both are due to static electricity, which also causes lightning.

Radio

Cooker

Kettle

CREATIVE CORNER

Sticky static

Rub a balloon on your hair and the balloon will stick to the wall. Rubbing removes tiny bits of electricity called electrons from the balloon, leaving it and your hair charged with electricity. Electrically charged things pull on other things, such as the wall. It is this pull that holds the balloon in place.

INTERNET LINKS: www.eia.gov/kids/energy.cfm?page=electricity_home-basics-k.cfm

Magnetism

Magnets are objects that pull on (attract) some kinds of metal. They also pull or push away (repel) other magnets. The area around a magnet that affects other things is called a magnetic field.

South

North

South

North

Magnets attract

South

North

North

South

Magnets repel

▶ Each magnet has a north and a south 'pole'. These are places where the magnetism is strongest. A north pole will attract a south pole. However, it will repel another north pole.

Compass

North pole

Magnetic field

Superscience

Maglev

Maglev is short for 'magnetic levitation'. Electromagnets are used to levitate the train so that it flies along a few centimetres above the track. Switching the electromagnets on and off in sequence can also propel the train forward.

▲ The Earth is a huge magnet. Small magnets called compasses line themselves up so that they point to the Earth's magnetic poles. People can use compasses to help them find their way.

VOCABULARY

dynamo
A device that makes electric currents from motion.

levitation
Lifting something up into the air without touching it.

Electromagnet

Michael Faraday (1791 – 1867)

Faraday was a scientist who made many discoveries about both electricity and magnetism. He discovered many new chemicals, and invented the electric motor and the dynamo.

▲ When electricity flows through a wire, the wire becomes a magnet. If the wire is wound around a piece of iron, it makes a much stronger magnet called an electromagnet. This one is used to pick up metal.

▶ An electromagnet can be made to spin in a magnetic field to make an electric motor. Vacuum cleaners and some toys contain electric motors.

INTERNET LINKS: www.bbc.co.uk/schools/scienceclips/ages/7_8/magnets_springs.shtml

Telecommunications

Telecommunication means sending messages by using electricity or radio signals. We cannot see radio signals. Mobile phones and most TVs use radio signals. Cable TV and landline phones use electrical signals that travel in wires.

▼ We can see objects because of the patterns of light that come from them. In a television studio, a camera changes the pattern of light from the newsreader into a pattern of electricity. Sounds are also changed into patterns of electricity, using microphones.

Mobile phones

The first mobile phones came on the market in the 1980s. Today, of about 6.5 billion people living on Earth, about half of them – more than 3 billion people – own a mobile phone. And many of them own more than one!

Dish transmitter

Newsreader

Camera

Transmitter mast

◄ The patterns of electricity are sent out by a 'transmitter' in the form of radio signals. Some transmitters are masts (right). Dish-shaped transmitters (above) aim signals at satellites.

Television studio

Underground cable

▼ Satellites in orbit around the Earth 'relay' TV signals. This means they receive signals from a transmitter on one part of the Earth and send them out to a receiver somewhere else.

Satellite

Guglielmo Marconi (1874–1937)
Marconi built the first successful 'radiotelegraph'. He used it to send messages through the air as radio signals. This meant that, for the first time, ships at sea could send and receive messages over long distances.

▼ Electrical TV signals need to be decoded. The decoder is either part of the TV, or a separate box. It changes the patterns of electricity back into the pictures and sounds of the newsreader again.

? WHAT DOES 'TELEVISION' MEAN
The word 'television' means 'far-seeing'. It comes from the Greek word *tele* which means 'far', and the Latin word *visio*, which means 'seeing'.

Digital television

Satellite aerial

Decoder

Yagi aerial

▶ Homes can receive TV signals in several ways. Signals that come from satellites are picked up by round aerials called satellite dishes. Signals from masts are picked up by 'Yagi' aerials. TV signals can also be sent through underground cables.

Underground cable

INTERNET LINKS: www.fcc.gov/cgb/kidszone/history_cellphone.html

Energy

Light, sound, heat, motion, electricity and magnetism are all types of energy. Without energy, nothing would happen and there would be no life. The food you eat gives you energy that you need to live.

Burning coal boils water

Coal from mines

Dynamo

WHERE DOES ENERGY GO TO?

Energy is never created or destroyed, but it can change from one type to another. In the end, all other types of energy turn into heat energy.

▲ Most of the Earth's energy comes from the Sun. Plants capture some of this energy in their leaves and use it to grow. Animals get their energy by eating the plants.

▲ Coal is burned to release heat energy. The heat boils water, producing jets of steam. A dynamo changes the 'kinetic' (motion) energy of the rushing steam to electricity.

◀ Gas, coal and oil are called fossil fuels. They are the remains of forests that were crushed and buried deep underground millions of years ago. We burn them to make heat and electricity.

Ancient forests

Coal seam

Coal mine

Albert Einstein (1879–1955)

Einstein discovered that mass and energy are really the same. He also explained what gravity is and showed that motion and gravity can slow down time. Einstein proved that light is broken up into tiny pieces called photons.

▲ Light bulbs usually waste a lot of electricity by turning it into heat energy. Modern 'low-energy' bulbs (above) make very little heat energy. They use less electricity to make the same amount of light energy.

Substation

Cables

Transformer

Factory

House

▲ Electricity from power stations is fed through transformers. These change the electricity so that it can move easily over long distances through cables (thick wires). Close to the factories and homes that use the electricity, there are substations. These change the electricity again, to make it easier for us to use.

Superscience

Nuclear power

The energy of the Sun, which we see as sunlight, comes from deep inside the Sun. This energy is set free when atoms change into other atoms. It is called nuclear energy. Some power stations use nuclear energy to make electricity. The most powerful bombs also use nuclear energy.

INTERNET LINKS: www.eia.doe.gov/kids • www.sciencemuseum.org.uk/energy

Wind and temperature

Temperature depends on many things – it is usually colder at night, in winter, the higher you are, and the closer you are to the poles. In many places, there is a direction from which the wind often blows. For instance, in northwest Europe the wind is often from the southwest. This is called the 'prevailing wind'.

▲ The strength of the wind is measured on something called the Beaufort Scale. In the picture above, there is a light breeze. This is force 2 on the Beaufort Scale. The wind speed is around 9km/h.

January: winter in the north, summer in the south

July: summer in the north, winter in the south

▲▶ The weather is usually hotter in the summer than in the winter. While it is winter in northern countries, it is summer in southern ones. These maps show the temperatures at different times of the year. The hottest areas are red, the coldest are grey.

WHAT IS FROST?
Sometimes the air is below 0°C (freezing point), and the ground is even colder. Water vapour from the air turns into white ice on the ground. This is called frost.

▲ This is a force 10 storm, with the wind blowing around 100km/h. The wind is strong enough to damage buildings and uproot trees.

▲ Now the storm has turned into a force 12 hurricane. The wind speed is around 130km/h. It is strong enough to destroy buildings. Hurricanes are very dangerous, but are rare in most parts of the world.

▲ When air cools, it becomes heavier and sinks. Warmed air rises, and cooler air moves in to take its place. These movements of the air are the winds.

CREATIVE CORNER

Keep a weather diary
Every day for a week, write down what the weather is doing – cloudy, rainy, cold etc. To find out about the wind, throw a leaf into the air. Use a compass to check which way it is blown. Winds that blow from the same direction often bring the same sort of weather.

Clouds and rain

Many clouds, such as cumulus and stratus, are made of millions of tiny water droplets. When these droplets stick together, they fall from the cloud as raindrops or snowflakes. High clouds are made of tiny pieces of ice.

WHAT IS FOG?
Fog is really cloud at ground-level. It forms when water vapour rises from damp ground or blows in from the sea. It cools and becomes cloud-like.

Clouds

Sun

Rain

Sea

Driest place on Earth
The Atacama desert, in Chile, is the driest place on Earth. In some parts of it, rain only falls every few centuries. The reason is that rain clouds release all their rain over high mountains before they reach the Atacama. The average rainfall in the area is just 1mm a year.

▲ The Sun turns water from the seas to vapour. This turns into clouds of water droplets. The winds blow the clouds over the land, and rain falls from them. Plants draw water from the ground and turn it into more vapour. All these processes make up the water cycle.

Cirrus

Altocumulus

Stratocumulus

Cumulus

Cumulonimbus

Nimbostratus

Stratus

▲ The main cloud types are cumulus, stratus and cirrus. Those that bring rain have the word 'nimbus' in their name, like the cumulonimbus storm cloud above. Cirrus clouds float high in the air, and cumulus and stratus are quite near the ground. Clouds at in-between heights have 'alto' in their name.

INTERNET LINKS: http://eo.ucar.edu/webweather/cloud3.html

Now you know!

▲ Magnets can both pull and push on other magnets. Magnets also pull on some metals.

▲ Everything is moving. Even when you seem to be standing still, you and the Earth are travelling through space.

▲ Temperature is a measure of how hot something is. Cold is a lack of heat.

▲ There are many different sorts of energy. They include light, sound, heat, electricity, motion and magnetism.

▲ All objects pull on all other objects with the force of gravity.

▲ Light is made of waves. We see waves of different lengths as different colours.

▲ Sounds are series of squashes in the air (or in water), called waves. The closer together these squashes are, the higher the pitch of the sound we hear.

▲ Most of the Earth's energy comes from the Sun. Some of this energy is locked up in coal, oil and gas until we burn these fuels.

The world of materials

The Earth, and everything on it, is made
of materials. So are the Sun, Moon and stars.
You are made of materials, too. All materials
are made of tiny things called atoms, that are
much too small to see. We need materials for
everything we do, from the food we eat to the
air we breathe and the clothes we wear.

Solids

Things that have fixed shapes, such as pieces of wood or stone, are called solids. In a solid, the atoms (see box below) hold on to each other strongly. This is why solids are hard to pull apart.

Diamond is the hardest natural solid. An artificial form of diamond is the hardest solid people have made.

Quartz crystals

Superscience

Atoms
Atoms are tiny things, much too small for you to see without a powerful microscope. All solids, liquids and gases are made up of atoms. A single drop of water is made of more than a billion trillion atoms.

▲ Many solids are made of shapes called crystals. Crystals form when lots of atoms stick to each other to make a pattern. Most crystals are too small to see.

◄ Natural materials are those that people collect, rather than make for themselves. Wood is a natural material. We use it for all sorts of things, such as burning, building, and making paper and furniture.

▶ Most sorts of metal are found mixed into rocks called ores (see page 79). But gold is found as a pure metal. It stays shiny for thousands of years.

Gold statue of Tutankhamun

◀ Solids can change into liquids when they get hot. This is called melting. Solid ice-cream turns into a liquid as it warms up.

▲ Materials made by people are called 'artificial'. People make them in the way they want. This girl is wearing waterproof artificial materials.

CREATIVE CORNER

Extraordinary eggs

Put an egg in a cup and cover it with vinegar. After a few days the eggshell will be soft. Eggshells are hard because they contain calcium. The vinegar has drawn the calcium out of the shell.

Liquids

Liquids are runny substances that spread out to cover the base of whatever container they are put into. They do this because the molecules in a liquid can slip past each other easily.

VOCABULARY

dissolve
To disappear into a liquid.

droplet
Tiny drop of a liquid such as water.

molecule
A group of atoms that hold together strongly.

◄ When water is heated, it boils and steams. Steam is a mixture of hot gas (that we cannot see) and clouds of hot water droplets.

► Mercury is the only metal that is a liquid when it is at room temperature.

Superscience

Liquid crystals
These crystals can be runny like liquids, but they can also make patterns like crystals (see page 66). These patterns can be controlled by electricity. Liquid crystals can be used to make television screens, like the one on the right.

▲ Blood is mostly water. It has sugars, gases and other materials dissolved in it. It also has cells (see page 99) floating in it. This person is giving blood that will be used to help someone else.

▶ Water, like that pouring down in this waterfall, is vital to all life on Earth. Plants suck it from the soil, animals drink it and fish swim in it. Clouds help to carry water right round the world.

▼ Things that we think of as solid, such as rocks, can turn into liquids if they get hot enough. The lava from this volcano is melted rock.

CREATIVE CORNER

Strange liquids

Half-fill a large glass with warm water. Pour in 2cm of cooking oil (the liquids will not mix). Add two spoonfuls of salt. The strange bubbles happen because the salt drags the oil down and then lets it float up again. After a while, all the salt disappears. It has dissolved in the water.

69

Gases

In a gas, the molecules are quite a long way away from each other compared to those in a solid or liquid. If a gas is put into a box, it will spread out to fill it. Most gases are transparent (clear).

John Dalton (1766–1844)
Dalton realized that gases expand (grow larger) when they get hotter. He also helped to develop the modern theory of atoms, compounds and elements (see page 72).

?
DO GASES SMELL?
Some gases smell quite a lot! Hydrogen sulphide makes rotten eggs and farts smell. Ammonia has a very strong smell, and is sometimes used to wake people who have fainted.

▲ An explosion happens when a lot of gas is made very quickly. Gunpowder is an explosive that was invented hundreds of years ago. To demolish (knock down) buildings, an explosive called TNT (trinitrotoluene) is often used. Nitroglycerine is a liquid that explodes if it is moved suddenly.

◄ Helium is a gas that is lighter than air. Because of this, a balloon filled with helium will rise up and float away through the air.

▲ Yeast is a tiny living thing. When mixed with flour and water, it makes carbon dioxide gas, which makes the mixture swell (left). When baked, the mixture becomes bread (right).

► Gases can dissolve in liquids. Drinks can be made fizzy by dissolving carbon dioxide in them.

► Gases become liquids when they cool. When air with a lot of water gas (called water vapour) in it touches a cool mirror, the vapour turns into tiny drops of liquid. They make the mirror cloudy.

CREATIVE CORNER

Make carbon dioxide

Pour vinegar into a small bottle so that is about a quarter full. Use a funnel to fill a balloon with bicarbonate of soda. Stretch the balloon over the bottle's top, and lift it so the soda falls into the bottle. The balloon will swell with carbon dioxide (CO_2) gas.

INTERNET LINKS: www.chem4kids.com/files/matter_gas.html

Elements

Everything is made of elements. Elements join together to make compounds. For example, water is a compound of the elements hydrogen and oxygen.

Pencil and graphite

Diamonds

◀ The same element can appear in different forms. Graphite and diamond are both forms of the element carbon, but diamond is hard and graphite is soft. Pencil leads contain graphite.

Superscience

Molecules

Molecules are joined together atoms (see page 66). Some, such as oxygen, are made of atoms of the same kind. Oxygen's molecules are made of two oxygen atoms. Other molecules are made of different atoms.

▶ The element neon is a gas at room temperature. It is used to make some light bulbs and glowing signs, such as this neon sign of a parrot.

Sodium

Chlorine

Salt

▲ Elements join to other elements to make compounds. Salt is a compound of sodium and chlorine. Sodium is a soft metal, chlorine is a poisonous gas.

Short-lived elements
There are 117 elements. Of these, 92 are natural. The other 25 are artificial – in other words, they have been made by people. Many of these artificial elements destroy themselves soon after they are made. Some last for less than one second!

Strontium chloride

Copper sulphate

Copper chloride

Sodium chloride

▲ When elements and compounds burn, they make coloured flames. The above compounds are all called salts. The salt that we eat is sodium chloride.

▲ Silicon can be combined with other elements to control the way electricity passes through it. This is why it is used to make microchips (see page 26).

Dmitri Mendeleev (1834–1907)
Mendeleev arranged the elements in a table according to their weights and the way they behaved. This is now called the Periodic Table.

INTERNET LINKS: http://elements.wlonk.com/Elements_Pics+Words_11x8.5.pdf

Chemical reactions

Materials made of one sort of molecule or atom are called chemicals. Water, salt, sugar and carbon dioxide are all chemicals. In a chemical reaction, chemicals change into other chemicals.

Cooked egg

▲ Heating can cause chemical reactions. Raw egg 'white' is clear, but when it is cooked it turns white. This reaction is irreversible – it cannot be undone.

Superscience

Forensics
Forensics means the use of science to help solve crimes. For example, chemical tests on the blood of a dead person can show if they were poisoned. Forensics can show how long ago the person died.

► Firework rockets contain a mixture of chemicals. These burn quickly, making gases that push the rockets up into the air. The colourful sparks are made by other burning chemicals.

Marie Curie (1867–1934)

Curie used chemistry to separate tiny amounts of an element called radium from many tonnes of an ore (see page 79) called pitchblende. Radium glows in the dark and can cause or treat some types of cancer.

▲ Candy floss is mostly sugar. Sucrose is a type of sugar. The chemical formula for sucrose is $C_{12}H_{22}O_{11}$. This tells us sucrose is made of carbon (C), hydrogen (H) and oxygen (O).

CREATIVE CORNER

Colourful chemistry

Ask an adult to chop some red cabbage, and pour very hot water onto it. After 20 minutes, spoon some of the liquid into lemon juice. Next put some onto bicarbonate of soda. Try other things, such as toothpaste or vinegar. Substances that turn cabbage water red are called acids. Those that turn it blue are called bases.

Air

The Earth is surrounded by the atmosphere, which is made of air. Air is a mixture of gases, and it also contains dust. Living things could not survive without the gases that make up air.

▶ If you travelled up in a rocket, you would find the air getting thinner. Finally, it would disappear completely. By then, the sky would be black instead of blue, and you would see stars all the time.

CAN YOU FIND?
1. Water
2. Clouds
3. A pie chart
4. Forests
5. A jumbo jet
6. A space shuttle

Meteor shower

Passenger jet

Nitrogen

Oxygen

Argon and carbon dioxide

Clouds

Glider

▲ Air is mostly nitrogen, with some oxygen. There are also small amounts of argon and carbon dioxide. When we breathe, it is only the oxygen that we use.

International
Space Station

Aurora
borealis

77

Antoine-Laurent de Lavoisier (1743–1794)

Lavoisier discovered that rusting, burning and breathing all use up oxygen. He also realized that materials never just disappear in a chemical reaction. They change into other materials.

Space shuttle

▶ Cars, factories and fires add chemicals to the air that can damage the health of living things. These chemicals are called pollutants. Some pollutants trap the Sun's heat. This makes the Earth get warmer.

CREATIVE CORNER

Invisible water

Fill a glass with ice-cubes. After a while, the outside will be damp. This is water, which has 'condensed' from the air. The air contains a great deal of water that we cannot see because it is in the form of a gas.

INTERNET LINKS: http://earthguide.ucsd.edu/earthguide/diagrams/atmosphere/index.html

Rock

A mineral is a solid that is made of a particular arrangement (pattern) of chemicals. Rocks are made of mixtures of minerals. The study of rocks is called geology.

Emerald

Amethyst

Citrine

Garnet

Aquamarine

▲ When one sort of rock changes to another, the new rock is called metamorphic. Marble is a metamorphic rock. Many statues are made of marble.

WHERE DOES SOIL COME FROM?
Soil is rock that has been broken into tiny pieces by the weather. Soil also contains water, air, tiny living things, and the broken-up remains of dead plants and animals.

◄ Granite is an igneous rock. Igneous rocks form when lava cools and hardens. This is a granite tor, which is a large piece of granite that sticks out of the ground.

▼ Gems (also known as 'precious stones') are attractive minerals. They are cut and polished, and used to make jewellery. Large gems are expensive, because they are hard to find.

Ruby

Topaz

Pink sapphire

Yellow sapphire

Diamond

The age of rocks

Most ancient rocks are buried deep underground, but in a few places they can be seen on the surface of the Earth. In 2008, researchers discovered rocks they believe are 4,280 million years old.

▲ Rocks that contain gems or metals which people find useful are called ores. Modern mining methods include the use of giant machines like this one. It is digging out rocks containing ore near the surface.

Stalagmite

Stalactite

▲ Limestone is a sedimentary rock. This means it forms from chemicals dissolved in water. Limestone caves contain stalagmites and stalactites.

CREATIVE CORNER

Make stalactites

Dissolve as much sugar as you can in warm water. Put a saucer between two glasses. Put one end of a 20cm-long piece of wool in each glass. Fill with the liquid. Stalactites, like those in limestone caves, will grow over a few days.

Bricks and building

Wood, bricks, stone and concrete
have been used for building over
thousands of years. Modern buildings,
especially large ones, are often made
using steel and concrete. Builders also
use other metals, plastic and glass.

CAN YOU FIND?
1. Two bridges
2. Skyscrapers
3. A road
4. A crane
5. Sand
6. A steel girder

▶ In modern cities, the main
buildings, roads, bridges and
railways are planned to work
together. This is so that
people are able to move
around safely and easily.

▲ Bricks are usually made from
clay. They are baked in an oven
to make them hard, and then stuck
together with mortar. Mortar is a
mixture of cement, sand and water.

The tallest building
The world's tallest building is the Burj Khalifa, which is a skyscraper in Dubai in the United Arab Emirates. It is more than 800m high.

▲ Here, a multi-storey steel and concrete building is being put up. Concrete is made of cement mixed with sand, water and other materials. Cement is mostly powdered limestone.

WHEN WERE BRICKS INVENTED?
Bricks were invented more than 9,000 years ago. They were not as strong as modern bricks, because they were dried by the sun, rather than in ovens.

Metals

Most metals are shiny, grey and heavy, and bend rather than snap. Most of the elements are metals, and electricity and heat pass easily through them. People use metals to make machines and other useful things.

▶ For more than 5,000 years, people have used shiny, hard-wearing metals to make coins and other things. Some metals are rare and are worth more than others.

Rusted iron

Gold

Brass (copper + zinc)

Superscience

Steel

Adding carbon and other elements to iron turns it into a stronger and more useful metal called steel. When metals are mixed with other elements, they are called alloys. Alloys are usually harder than the metals they are made from.

Copper

Silver

Bronze
(copper + tin)

Pewter (tin + copper
+ antimony + lead)

83

CAN YOU FIND?
1. 4 goblets
2. 10 plates
3. 3 lids
4. A latch
5. A handle
6. 3 candlesticks

Polished
copper

Tarnished
copper

CREATIVE CORNER

Making rust

Line an old tray with kitchen towels. Put some unwanted metal things, such as nails, scissors, nail files and pan-scourers on top. Sprinkle with salt and lemon juice, and leave for a few days. Some of the things will go rusty. Rust is a compound of iron and oxygen.

INTERNET LINKS: www.brainpop.com/science/matter/metals/preview.weml

Wood and paper

Wood is a natural material that is very useful for many purposes. This is because it is strong, not very heavy and easy to cut to shape. It can also be treated so that it lasts a long time.

▶ Paper is designed for the way it is used. Toilet paper breaks down easily, envelopes are strong and printed paper is smooth.

▲ This is a teak tree (above right). Teak is a hard, tough wood. It is used to make the decks of boats, which need to stand up to salt water and bad weather.

▲ Oak trees like this one are often used for building the frames of houses (right). Oak is strong, fairly light in weight and lasts for a long time.

Superscience

Plywood

Plywood is made by gluing together thin layers of wood. This makes the wood stronger and less likely to 'warp' (change shape). Plywood can also be shaped easily. It is used to make many things including furniture, boats and buildings.

▶ Paper is made mainly from wood. Wood gets its strength from a material called cellulose. The cellulose gives strength to the paper as well.

Wood is made into woodchips.

It is mixed with chemicals.

The paper is pressed to remove liquids and then laid flat to dry.

The finished paper is made into large rolls for transport.

CREATIVE CORNER

Paper strengths

Collect different sorts of paper and guess how strong they are. Cut a 10cm square from each piece of paper and tear it in half. Write down how easy each was to tear. Were your guesses right? Some paper is made to be weak so it can be broken down easily, but some is strong.

Glass

Glass is made mostly of oxygen and an element called silicon. Unlike most solids, some glass is transparent (clear). So we use it to make windows and containers.

◄ When glass is heated, it becomes soft and easy to shape. Then it can be blown to make hollow, rounded shapes.

Superscience

Toughened glass

The main problem with most glass is that it is brittle – that is, it will break if it is hit. However, glass can be toughened. It has to be heated very gently and carefully, or it can have potassium added to it.

▲ Glass can be coloured by adding metal compounds to it. This stained-glass window was made by joining pieces of coloured glass using strips made of lead. Stained-glass windows can often be seen in churches.

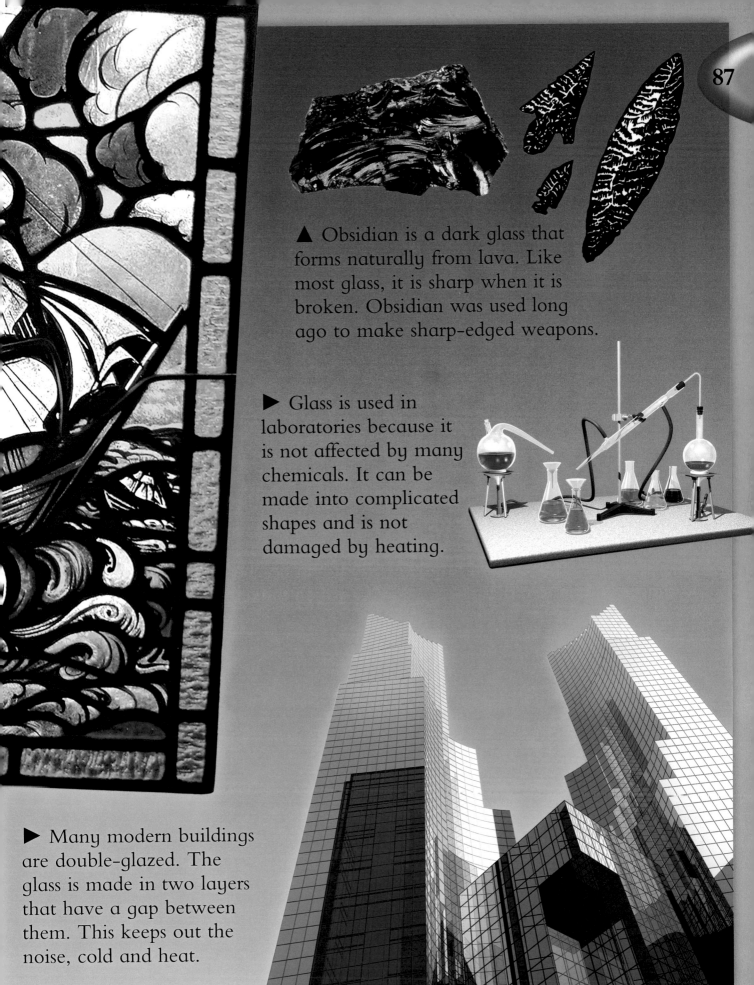

▲ Obsidian is a dark glass that forms naturally from lava. Like most glass, it is sharp when it is broken. Obsidian was used long ago to make sharp-edged weapons.

► Glass is used in laboratories because it is not affected by many chemicals. It can be made into complicated shapes and is not damaged by heating.

► Many modern buildings are double-glazed. The glass is made in two layers that have a gap between them. This keeps out the noise, cold and heat.

Oil and fuel

A fuel is something that is used up to release energy (see page 58). Oil, coal and some types of gas are all used as fuels. Oil is also used to make useful chemicals.

(see page 58)

IS BURNING FUEL A PROBLEM?

The oil, coal and gas that we burn makes the world warmer and dirtier. So we also make power in other ways – from falling water, waves, sunlight, wind and from splitting atoms too.

▲ Coal is the remains of ancient forest plants. It is found underground, and is removed by mining (see page 58). Coal is usually burned in power stations to make electricity.

(see page 58)

▲ Some types of gas are used as fuels. Propane gas is used in barbeques and some engines. It can be changed to a liquid, which makes it easy to store.

Superscience

Organic chemistry

Organic chemistry is the study of those chemicals made mainly of carbon and hydrogen. There are an enormous number of these chemicals, some of which can be made from oil. People, and all other animals as well as plants, are made of organic chemicals.

▶ Wood has been used as a fuel for thousands of years. When wood (or anything else) is burned, oxygen gas is used up and carbon dioxide gas is made.

Carbon dioxide gas

Oxygen gas

Petrol

Candles

Lubricating oil

Paint

◀ The oil that comes out of the ground is called 'crude oil'. It is a mix of different chemicals, which can be separated. They may be used as they are, or turned into other things.

▶ Oil and gas are found under the ground. When the ground is under the sea, 'rigs' are used to reach the oil and gas. Some rigs are attached to the ocean floor, but others can float on the surface.

CAN YOU FIND?

1. A tower
2. Two cranes
3. A helicopter
4. A helipad
5. The horizon

INTERNET LINKS: www2.illinoisbiz.biz/coal/virtualtour/index.html

Plastic and rubber

Most plastics and rubbers are made of polymers. Polymers are long, thin molecules (see page 72), each made of thousands of atoms. There are natural and artificial rubbers, but all plastics are artificial.

Plastic blood

When someone is hurt, their blood can be replaced with blood that is taken from other people. However, artificial blood, which contains plastic molecules, keeps much longer.

◄ Lots of things are made of plastic. Some plastics are made very thin, to wrap things. Others can be filled with hot drinks or put in the oven without melting. And some are strong enough to make furniture or buildings.

◄ Most plastics last for a long time, so getting rid of them can be a problem. But plastic bottles and bags can be turned into other things, such as water pipes. This is called recycling.

◀ These divers are wearing wet suits. A thin layer of water is trapped between the suit and the skin, to keep the divers warm. Wet suits are made of neoprene, which is an artificial rubber.

Rubber tree

Rubber

CAN YOU FIND?
1. A diving suit
2. Oxygen tanks
3. A PVC boat
4. A plastic torch
5. Liquid rubber

▲ Natural rubber is produced by rubber trees. To make it last longer, natural rubber is heated with chemicals such as sulphur. Then it can be used to make useful things such as wellington boots for the rain.

▲ This boat is inflatable, which means it is blown up with air. Inflatable boats are light and easy to carry. They are often made of a plastic called PVC (polyvinyl chloride).

Fibres and dyes

Most of your clothes are made from fibres, which are woven or knitted together. Your clothes are coloured by chemicals called dyes. Fibres and dyes are used for lots of other things too.

Sheep

Woollen jumper

▼ Pens contain inks, which are coloured liquids that dry quickly. Clothes are coloured with similar liquids, called dyes. Natural dyes usually lose their colour much faster than artificial ones.

Denim jacket

Cotton plant

▲ Many clothes are made from cotton or wool. Both are natural fibres. Cotton comes from a plant, and wool comes from sheep.

Superscience

Optical fibres

Glass can be made into very thin, long pieces called optical fibres. Light can be sent along these fibres, even when they are bent. Optical fibres are often used for sending signals between computers and for making glowing decorations.

Nylon

Many of the clothes we wear are made of artificial fibres, such as nylon. Nylon is a strong fibre, so it can be used to make carpets and many other things. The bristles in your toothbrush are probably made of nylon.

▲ Some boats are made of plastic with very thin glass fibres mixed into it. This material is called fibreglass. It is very strong and light.

▶ Silk is a natural fibre made by silkworms and spiders. Some spiders use silk to make webs to catch insects. Some clothes are made from silk.

▲ Sweets are coloured by adding food dyes to them. Cochineal is a red food dye made from ground-up insects!

CREATIVE CORNER

Splitting ink

Halfway up an oblong of kitchen paper about 15cm long, make big dots using marker pens. Put about 5cm of water in a glass and stand the paper in it. The water will slowly smear out the dots, showing that some inks are made of different colours.

INTERNET LINKS: http://nobelprize.org/educational_games/chemistry/plastics/index.html

Engineering

Engineers use science to design and build useful things, such as bridges, cars and computers. To do this, they often make artificial materials with the properties that they need, such as lightness, strength or smoothness.

▲ Chemicals that are needed in large quantities, such as fertilizers, plastics or fuel, are made in large chemical factories (or 'plants').

▶ Engineers build planes from many artificial materials. The windows are made of toughened glass and the airframes contain the lightweight metal aluminium. The fuel is designed specially to help them run smoothly.

The longest tunnel
The world's longest tunnel is the Seikan railway tunnel in Japan. It is an amazing 23.3km long and most of it is under the sea. It is also the deepest railway tunnel in the world.

VOCABULARY

airframe
The parts of a plane other than its engines.

factory
A building or group of buildings where things are made.

fertilizer
A chemical that helps plants to grow.

▲ When the same thing is made over and over again, like bread in this factory, this is called mass production. It is usually done by complicated machinery that is controlled by a computer.

Superscience

Smart materials

New materials are being invented all the time. The lenses of some sunglasses that people wear today are made of a special plastic. It gets darker the sunnier it is outside. There are also some alloys that can be twisted from one shape to another, and then go back to their first shape when they are heated. Both these materials are described as 'smart'.

Now you know!

◄ Everything is made of tiny things called atoms, that are much too small to see.

► A chemical is a material made of one sort of molecules or atoms. Salt is a chemical. Its scientific name is sodium chloride.

► Many clothes are made of fibres. These fibres may be natural, such as cotton, or artificial, such as nylon.

▲ Some materials, such as gold, are called elements. Other materials, such as water, are compounds. Compounds are joined-together elements.

▲ Materials can be solids, liquids or gases. Often, a solid material will turn into a liquid if it gets hot enough. When it gets hotter still, it turns into a gas.

▲ People use natural materials, such as wood and rubber. They also use artificial materials, such as plastic and concrete.

▲ The air is a mixture of gases. One of them is oxygen, the gas we need to live.

▲ Atoms can join together to make molecules. Two atoms of hydrogen can join with one atom of oxygen to make one molecule of water.

Living things

You are a human, just one of the millions of kinds of living things that live together on the Earth. Living things are amazingly different from one another. For example, a blade of grass is nothing like an eagle. However, the same scientific laws explain how both of them live.

What is life?

A tree and an ant seem to have nothing in common. But there are seven things that they both do, as do all other living things: they move, breathe, eat, produce waste, react, grow and reproduce.

▲ Many animals, including people, sleep. While they are asleep, the processes inside them, such as breathing, continue. These processes are what keep animals and plants alive.

▶ Every living thing can move. Some, such as these flamingos, can fly, while others swim, burrow, walk or crawl. Plants move too, but usually only in one place – for example, flowers open up in sunlight.

CAN YOU FIND?
1. leaves
2. two tongues
3. wings
4. roots
5. beaks
6. lily pads

Superscience

Cells

Every living thing is made of one or more tiny building-blocks that are called cells. You are made of trillions of them. There are many sorts of cells, such as blood cells and muscle cells. Some cells are built up into tissues, such as muscle tissue. Organs, such as the heart or stomach, are made of tissues.

▼ Animals, like this giraffe, need to breathe and eat food. Later it will excrete the waste from the food. Plants also 'breathe' and eat, taking what they need from air and water.

◄ Living things react to whatever happens to them. This parsley grows towards sunlight, because it needs the light to help it grow.

▲ All living things grow. Vegetables such as cauliflowers, cabbages and beans go through several stages of growth, from seed through seedling to adult plant.

▲ Living things reproduce, which means that they make new living things that are similar to them. Most snakes reproduce by laying eggs.

INTERNET LINKS: www.uen.org/core/science/sciber/sciber3/stand-2/1a.shtml

The five kingdoms

Every living thing is a member of a species. Similar species are grouped together. The five main groups are called kingdoms. Your species is *Homo sapiens,* part of the animal kingdom.

Carl Linnaeus (1707–78)

Linnaeus invented a way of naming species. He gave each one a two-word Latin name. For example, a horse is *Equus caballus.*

▶ All plants are able to take in and use sunlight. Fungi cannot do this. Instead they feed on living or dead animals or plants, or on their waste products.

Plants

Fungi

Flowering

Non-flowering

Cranesbill

Mosses

Fly agaric mushroom

VOCABULARY
monerans
The simplest living things, with only one cell; sometimes divided into two kingdoms.
protists
Mostly single-celled living things that are sometimes brightly coloured.

No one knows how many individual living things there are on Earth, but there are at least 5 million trillion trillion.

Monerans

Animals

Protists

With backbone

Without backbone

Salmonella bacterium

Green lizard

Slime moulds

Octopus

Animals

Animals are either 'vertebrates', which have backbones, or they are 'invertebrates', which do not. Mammals, birds, reptiles, fish and amphibians are vertebrates. Molluscs and arthropods are just two of the many types of invertebrates.

▲ This poison dart frog is an amphibian. Amphibians are born underwater. Later, their bodies change so that they can live on land.

Gills

Giant insects

The heaviest insect is the goliath beetle. The larvae (maggots) of this beetle weigh up to 100g – heavier than a tomato! Insects cannot get much bigger than this, because they breathe through their skins. Larger animals need lungs or gills to get the oxygen they need to live.

▲ Fish live underwater and breathe through gills. Most are covered in scales and move around using fins. This fish is a great white shark, which lives by hunting smaller animals.

▶ Mammals feed their young with milk. Most mammals have live young, but a few mammals lay eggs. This field mouse is a mammal, and so are you.

▶ Reptiles are covered in scales, and most of them lay eggs. Lizards, tortoises and crocodiles are all reptiles, and so are snakes such as this green tree viper.

There are over one million animal species. Most are insects and 99 per cent are smaller than bumblebees. New ones are found every year.

▲ Arthropods are a very large group of animals. All insects, crabs and spiders are arthropods. Insects, such as this stag beetle, all have six legs and a hard outer shell.

▶ All birds lay eggs, and have feathers, beaks and wings – though not all birds can fly. These are lovebirds, which live in Africa. They are called lovebirds because pairs stay together.

▲ Snails, squid, slugs and octopuses are different kinds of mollusc. Many molluscs, such as this snail, have shells that protect them from their enemies and from drying out.

CREATIVE CORNER

Make an animal collage

Find the largest piece of paper you can and draw or stick pictures of your favourite animals onto it – you might find pictures on the internet, or perhaps take your own photographs. Can you find at least one of each of the types of animal on this page?

INTERNET LINKS: www.nhm.ac.uk/kids-only/naturecams/

Plants

Plants are living things, like animals. They are made of cells and react to things around them. Plants get their food from sunlight, and most plants grow from seeds.

WHY ARE MOST PLANTS GREEN?
Plants are coloured green by the chemical chlorophyll. This captures some of the energy (see page 58) from sunlight. The plant uses the energy to live and grow.

◄ This cone contains seeds. It is made by a pine tree, which is a type of conifer. Most conifers are evergreen – they have leaves all year long. They grow as either trees or shrubs.

► Horsetails were common millions of years ago, in the time of the dinosaurs. Most have now died out, but we find many remains (called fossils) in rocks. Horsetails have no flowers.

▼ There are many species of flowering plant. They grow from seeds, and have spread widely all over the world. These are flowers on a magnolia tree.

▼ This tree trunk is covered in mosses and climbing ivy. Mosses are small plants that grow close together. Ivy either creeps along the ground or climbs trees or walls. It is an evergreen, which means it stays green all year.

Maidenhair fern

The oldest trees

The oldest type of tree is the bristlecone pine, which can live for up to 5,000 years. One famous old bristlecone pine grew in eastern Nevada, in the USA. It was called Prometheus and was cut down by mistake in 1964.

▲ Ferns usually live in damp areas in woods and forests. They grow from spores. Like conifers and flowering plants, ferns contain tubes that move chemicals and water around inside them.

▶ The roots and stems of this water lily are underwater, but its leaves and flowers float on the surface. Many plants live underwater, but always near the surface where there is sunlight.

Eating and breathing

To survive, all living things must take in and give out gases (breathe). They also need energy. Animals get their energy from eating other living things. Plants get their energy from sunlight.

VOCABULARY

photosynthesis
The process in which plants take in light and chemicals to make other chemicals.

respiration
Breathing, or the way that animals get energy from food.

▶ During the day, leaves absorb carbon dioxide gas, water and sunlight. From these, they make the chemicals the plant needs. They give out oxygen gas and water.

Leaf surfaces are waxy to prevent water loss

Leaf cells are packed with chloroplasts, which contain chlorophyll

Blade of a leaf grows from a stalk

▶ Underwater animals get oxygen from the water through gills. Land animals get oxygen from the air, using their lungs. Tadpoles start life with gills. They then develop lungs as they become frogs.

Frog

Tadpole

William Harvey (1578–1657)
Harvey discovered that blood flows round the body, pumped by the heart. Now we know that blood carries oxygen, carbon dioxide and food chemicals.

▲ Many animals, such as zebra, are herbivores (plant-eaters). Lions are carnivores (meat-eaters). Animals that can eat both meat and plants are called omnivores. People are omnivores. A very few plants, such as the Venus flytrap (see page 108), eat animals.

Oxygen

Respiration

Photosynthesis

Carbon dioxide

▶ All over the world, especially in the seas, plants give out oxygen. Animals such as howler monkeys (above) breathe in oxygen and breathe out carbon dioxide, which the plants take in. At night, plants also take in some oxygen.

Moving

Both plants and animals can move parts of themselves. For instance, some plants move their leaves to face the Sun. Most animals, and some very small and simple plants, can also move from place to place.

▲ Most animals, like this earthworm, can move because they have muscles. When an animal wants to move, it sends a signal from its brain to a muscle, which gets shorter and the animal moves.

▲ Many plants can move their leaves, or open and close their flowers. This poppy opens its flowers during the day and closes them at night. Some plants curl their stems around objects to climb upwards.

Snappy eater
Plants usually move too slowly to see, but the Venus flytrap moves almost too fast to see. It has special leaves that snap shut in only one-tenth of a second when a fly lands on them! Then the plant digests the fly.

▼ Large animals such as tigers and wild pigs have skeletons inside them. These are made of bones with muscles attached. Muscles often work in groups, pulling the bones in different directions.

Most birds, many insects, and some other animals can fly. The bodies of swifts (left) have evolved to allow them to glide and swoop through the air very quickly. They need to do this to catch flying insects and escape from enemies.

WHAT IS THE FASTEST FISH?

The fastest fish is the sailfish, which can swim at more than 100km/h. This is about the same speed as a car travels on a motorway.

Insects and many other small animals such as scorpions (above) have skeletons on the outsides of their bodies, a bit like suits of armour. Muscles for movement are attached to the insides of the skeletons. As scorpions grow, their skeletons split open and fall off several times.

Fish often have smooth shapes to help them slip easily through the water. Many fish have fins, which they use to push themselves along and to steer. Many also have 'swim bladders', which they fill with air to move upwards through the water.

Reproduction

Reproduction makes new living things. Many plants and animals reproduce sexually, which means that two parents are needed to make new offspring. Others can reproduce on their own.

◀ Very simple creatures, such as this amoeba, reproduce by splitting in half. When an animal or plant reproduces on its own like this, we call it asexual reproduction.

▲ To make a new person, a sperm cell from a man 'fertilizes' (joins with) an egg cell from a woman. The egg cell grows into a baby inside the woman's body, in her womb.

Pregnant father
Unlike other animals, the male seahorse gives birth instead of the female. The male fertilizes the female's eggs, which she then lays inside the male. Up to 2,000 babies, called 'fry', are born a few weeks later.

◀ Female mammals produce milk from their bodies, which they use to feed their newborn babies. People usually only have one baby at a time, but rabbits are born in groups called litters. Baby rabbits drink their mother's milk for about one month.

▲ Dandelion seeds have a feathery 'parachute', which the wind blows, so they spread over wide areas. Each dandelion makes many seeds, because few land on soil where they can grow.

▲ Many plants, such as this hibiscus, reproduce sexually. Cells from male plants are sometimes carried to female plants by insects or birds, such as this ruby-throated hummingbird. This is called pollination.

Superscience

Hybrids

When one type of animal or plant is bred with another, a hybrid is produced. A mule is a hybrid of a male donkey and a female horse. Modern wheat is a hybrid of different types of grass.

▶ Many animals lay eggs from which their young hatch. Crocodiles protect their eggs until they hatch, and then guard the young carefully. Even so, most of the young die, which is why so many eggs are laid.

INTERNET LINKS: http://library.thinkquest.org/C004535/reproduction.html

Growth

Eggs hatch
after 4 days

Caterpillar lives
for 2 weeks

Every living thing grows from a single cell. Many keep growing until they die. As well as putting energy into growing, some animals also learn skills, such as hunting, as they become adults.

▼ Flowering plants grow from seeds. Seeds contain enough food for the young plant to grow a root and its first leaves. These first leaves often look very different to those that appear later.

Superscience

Nature and nurture

The way living things develop depends partly on their genes ('nature') and partly on what happens to them ('nurture'). The skills of high-jumpers are nurtured by training. However, it is mostly their genes that make them tall.

A runner bean plant develops from a seed

▼ Baby swans, and many other water birds, follow the first animal they see when they are born. Usually, this is one of the parents, but if it is a person or another animal, the babies will follow them.

Chrysalis forms

Chrysalis lasts for 2 weeks

Butterfly emerges

Butterfly flies away

▲ Some animals change shape completely as they grow, through 'metamorphosis'. This monarch butterfly began life as an egg. The caterpillar later changed into a chrysalis. The adult butterfly hatched from this.

Tree rings
When trees are cut down, light and dark rings can be seen inside them. A new light ring appears each summer, when the tree grows faster. Counting the rings gives the tree's age.

VOCABULARY

cells
The tiny structures from which living things are built.

genes
Instructions that tell a cell how to grow and function.

▶ Complicated animals such as people take many years to grow into adults. So they live in family groups, where the adults look after the children.

Life began in the seas, from chemical reactions.

Evolution

All living things have certain 'characteristics' that they pass on to their children. Over time, nature 'selects' characteristics – such as cleverness or sharp teeth – that make survival more likely. This is called evolution.

▼ The evolution of today's animals, plants and people took thousands of millions of years. For most of that time, life existed only in the seas.

Gregor Mendel (1822–84)
Many characteristics of living things occur in just two ways. For example, pea flowers are either purple or white. Mendel showed how such characteristics are inherited from parents.

Dinosaurs were the most successful animals for 160 million years.

▶ Labradors have a pair of genes that controls their coat colour. Puppies inherit one coat-colour gene from each parent. The puppy is light-coloured only if both are light-coat genes. If there is one of each, or both are dark, the puppy is dark.

Superscience

DNA

The genetic information that makes you the way you are is stored in huge molecules (see page 72) of a chemical called DNA. Your DNA is a mix of the DNA from both your parents. Every part of your body contains DNA.

People evolved from ape-like creatures.

▲ Darwin (see page 124) discovered that the 'best' living things survive, but what is 'best' varies. Each of these finches survives on a different island because it has evolved the best beak for the food available.

INTERNET LINKS: www.nhm.ac.uk/nature-online/life/dinosaurs-other-extinct-creatures/dino-directory/timeline.dsml

Animal senses

Animals' senses tell them about the world, helping them find food, escape enemies, learn and communicate. The main senses are sight, hearing, touch, smell and taste. Not every animal has all these senses.

Pit

▲ Taste tells animals whether something is good to eat. Different tastes are caused by different chemicals in food. Our tongues can detect these chemicals. This pit viper tastes the air to track down food.

▲ Many animals recognize each other, and their homes, by smell. Smells are caused by chemicals that float through the air. This St Bernard rescue dog can sniff out people lost in the snow.

Seeing heat

Some animals have senses that we do not. A pit viper's 'pits' (see above) can sense warm objects. This means it can hunt mice in the dark. Other animals can sense electricity or magnetism, or they can see ultraviolet light, which is invisible to humans.

▲ Earthworms can detect danger by feeling the earth wobble when animals walk across it. Animals have different detectors in their skins to feel pressure (see page 44), heat, cold and pain. Your whole body is covered in these.

▼ Many animals, such as this great horned owl, use their excellent eyesight to help them hunt. Having two eyes allows animals to judge distances. Not all animals can see in colour as humans can.

▼ Fennec foxes use hearing to detect danger and to communicate with each other. Having two ears means animals can work out where a sound is coming from.

CREATIVE CORNER

Map your tongue

People detect the main tastes (bitter, sour, salty and sweet) with different parts of the tongue. Dip a cotton bud into honey and touch different parts of your tongue with it. Mark on a drawing where the taste is strongest. Repeat with coffee, lemon juice and salty water.

Bitter

Sour

Salty

Sweet

Brains and control

Animals control their bodies with their brains. Clever animals, such as people, have big, complicated brains. Only people can really talk, but most animals communicate (give messages to each other) in other ways.

Speed of reaction
If you touch something hot, your hand jerks away in under a second. For very fast reactions like this there is no time to involve the brain – the nerves do the job more quickly on their own.

Brain

Nerves

Spinal cord

▲ One sign of intelligence in an animal is its ability to use a tool, as this woodpecker finch is doing. The bird uses twigs to dig out grubs. Tool-users are mammals or birds.

◀ The brain controls the body through the nerves. The nerves go to muscles, which move when the brain tells them to. Nerves also carry information from the senses (see page 116) to the brain.

▲ Birds like these Canada geese often fly in formation. Each keeps an eye on its neighbours to make sure the pattern stays the same. They call to each other as they fly.

▼ Birds, such as this male peacock, often make beautiful displays to attract a mate (below left). This is to show that the males are strong and healthy and will make good parents.

▲ Bees tell each other where food is by dancing in a figure of eight pattern. The dance shows the direction of the food, compared to the direction of the Sun.

▼ When angry, cats make their fur stand on end so that they look bigger. They also show their teeth and hiss. This tells the dog the cat is best left alone.

CREATIVE CORNER

Bird song

Listen to and record birds when you are out walking. Then listen to the bird songs on the website below and use them to identify and write down the birds you have heard. Birds sing to tell others to keep out of their territories, or to warn of danger.

INTERNET LINKS: www.open.ac.uk/Nature_Trail/Birds.htm

Attack and defence

Most animals and plants have enemies that want to eat them, so they have to defend themselves. Hunting animals need to attack their prey, or they will starve.

◄ Some snakes inject venom (poison) into their prey or enemies. They bite and squeeze venom through their hollow fangs. This cobra can spit its venom to blind an attacker.

► The rhinoceros is a plant-eater, and uses its horn only to defend itself. The horn is made of keratin, the same substance as human fingernails.

◄ Scorpions have tails containing stings. The venom in this sting is used to attack and paralyse prey. It is also used by the scorpion to defend itself.

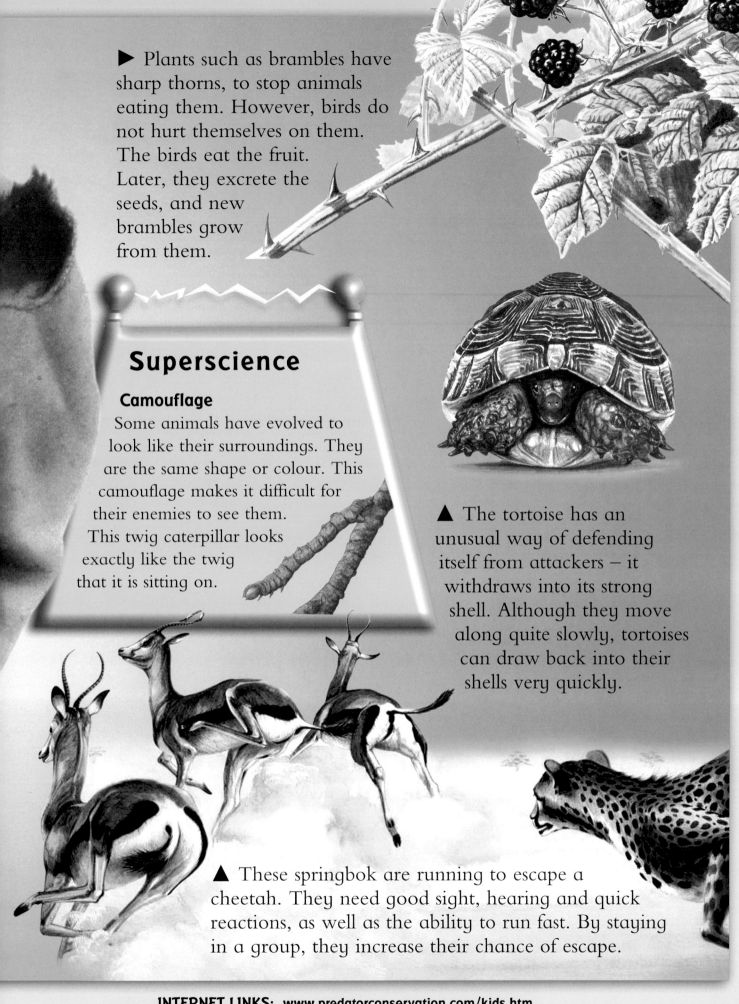

▶ Plants such as brambles have sharp thorns, to stop animals eating them. However, birds do not hurt themselves on them. The birds eat the fruit. Later, they excrete the seeds, and new brambles grow from them.

Superscience

Camouflage

Some animals have evolved to look like their surroundings. They are the same shape or colour. This camouflage makes it difficult for their enemies to see them. This twig caterpillar looks exactly like the twig that it is sitting on.

▲ The tortoise has an unusual way of defending itself from attackers – it withdraws into its strong shell. Although they move along quite slowly, tortoises can draw back into their shells very quickly.

▲ These springbok are running to escape a cheetah. They need good sight, hearing and quick reactions, as well as the ability to run fast. By staying in a group, they increase their chance of escape.

INTERNET LINKS: www.predatorconservation.com/kids.htm

Medicine

Living things have an amazing ability to recover from damage or illness. However, they sometimes need the help of medicine, first to find out what is wrong, and then to help them recover.

Living longer
There have been many amazing advances in medicines and medical care over the last 50 years. This has meant that people live longer. Today, there are people all over the world who live twice as long as their ancestors did, just 100 years ago.

◀ Some plants contain natural medicines. Medicine made from this foxglove can be used to help people who have heart problems. It is called digitalin.

▶ Veterinary surgeons ('vets') help animals stay healthy and treat them when they are ill. This vet is checking a baby giraffe's ears to make sure that it has not got a hearing problem.

▲ In countries such as Australia, it is often difficult for doctors to reach sick people by road. Instead, flying doctors arrive by plane, either to treat people or to fly them to hospital.

Louis Pasteur (1822–95)
Pasteur discovered a way to stop people catching a deadly disease called rabies. He also found out how to treat milk to make it safe to drink, and helped to show that diseases are caused by germs.

Superscience

Vaccination

Most disease germs are either bacteria (see page 125) or viruses. If a person is given specially weakened germs in a vaccination, their body gets used to them. The person will then be able to fight off the full-strength version of the disease.

▲ People often visit clinics where they can be treated for illnesses, have their health checked and receive vaccinations. When people are seriously ill, they go to hospital.

▶ Antibiotics are medicines that cure illnesses such as scarlet fever, which are caused by bacteria. Penicillin is an antibiotic medicine that is made from a fungus (right).

INTERNET LINKS: www.bbc.co.uk/cbbc/games/vet-set-go-game

Habitats and homes

Every type of animal and plant survives best in a particular place. This is called its habitat. Many animals also have homes that they either find or build.

Chamber

Queen

▲ Ants live underground. Worker ants dig out chambers in the earth connected by tunnels. The ant hills are used to store food, protect the queen ant and raise her young.

► Deep underwater there are volcanic vents. The warmth from these vents allows tube worms (the rod-like shapes), crabs, limpets and the creatures they eat to survive, These living things and their habitat together make up an 'ecosystem'.

Charles Darwin (1809–82)
Darwin explained that the animals and plants that cope best with their enemies and habitats survive. These living things evolve (change slowly) over many generations until they are perfect for their habitats.

► Many birds, such as this weaver bird, lay their eggs and raise their young in nests that they build from leaves, twigs or other things. They may line the nests with their own feathers for warmth.

◄ People have changed the world by building cities. Some animals, such as foxes, have moved in and adapted to this. It is easier for them to find food in the cities than in the wild.

► Humans make their own homes, often living in family groups. Dogs and cats make their homes with them. So do less welcome animals, such as cockroaches, mice and rats.

Living in hot water
Some tiny bacteria (members of the moneran kingdom, see page 101) live in hot springs, in water that is nearly boiling! They cannot survive at cooler temperatures.

Conservation

Around the world, many types of animals and plants are becoming extinct (dying out). The activities of humans are often to blame. However, today, many people are working hard to protect the remaining species.

Mass extinction
About 251 million years ago, most living things on our planet died. No one is sure why. This event is called a mass extinction. There was another mass extinction that killed off the dinosaurs about 65 million years ago.

▲ Forests provide a home to many plants and animals, so when a forest is destroyed, many species are at risk. The trees are cut down for their wood, or so that people can use the land for building or farming.

◀ The dodo became extinct when people took over its habitat. Over 99 per cent of all animal and plant species that have ever lived are now extinct.

▲ When the air, land or water are affected by chemicals or other waste matter, animals and plants living there may die. This is called pollution. Some pollution is caused by industry (see page 94).

▶ Siberian tigers are an endangered species, which means they risk becoming extinct. During the 20th century, they almost died out because they were hunted, but conservation measures have increased their numbers.

◀ African elephants were hunted for the ivory in their tusks. Now, many live in special safe areas called wildlife reserves and the sale of ivory is against the law.

CREATIVE CORNER

Save the environment
There are lots of things you can try:

• Make gifts instead of buying them.
• Walk or cycle to school instead of going by car.
• Put up nest boxes for wild birds.
• Grow herbs, fruit or vegetables.
• Join a conservation group locally.

Now you know!

▲ Every living thing is made of one or more cells.

▲ All living things move, breathe, eat, excrete, react, reproduce and grow.

▲ There are five kingdoms of life on our planet, Earth.

► Children are similar to both their parents because the similarities are passed on to them by their parents' genes.

▲ Each type of living thing has evolved to live in its own habitat.

▲ Different kinds of living things live together in ecosystems.

◄ Many living things are in danger of dying out altogether like the dodo.

▼ Living things evolved from chemicals over many millions of years.

Space

The Earth is enormous, yet it is only
a tiny dot in the whole vast Universe.
Using telescopes, rockets and robots,
people have found out many
things about planets, stars and
galaxies. But the Universe
is still full of mysteries.

The Universe

The Universe is everything that exists, and it stretches on endlessly. It contains billions of billions of stars, with trillions of kilometres of empty space between them. As well as the stars, planets and other objects that we can see, the Universe contains mysterious things called dark matter and dark energy.

▶ Stars are grouped into galaxies, many containing billions of stars. This picture shows a distant part of the Universe that contains many galaxies. Galaxies are grouped into clusters, and clusters into superclusters.

Superscience

The Big Bang

In the 1920s, scientists discovered that the Universe is growing bigger all the time. This means that, long ago, it must have been far smaller than it is today. The Universe began suddenly, about 13,700 million years ago, in a burst of energy called the Big Bang.

▶ On dark, cloudless nights, a fuzzy band of light arches across the sky. This is our galaxy, the Milky Way. The Sun, the Earth, the Moon and all the stars we can see with the naked eye are all part of this galaxy.

? IS THERE LIFE ELSEWHERE?

Most scientists think that life exists elsewhere in the Universe. They have sent radio messages and spaceships to try and find it.

▲ Many galaxies, such as the Whirlpool Galaxy, have spiral shapes. The bright patch on the right is a smaller galaxy, which passed through the Whirlpool, and caused stars to form there.

Edwin Hubble (1889–1953)

Edwin Hubble discovered that the Milky Way is not the only galaxy in the Universe. He and other scientists showed that almost all galaxies are moving away from each other, which means that the Universe is getting larger.

INTERNET LINKS: http://resources.schoolscience.co.uk/PPARC/bang/bang.htm

The Solar System

The Earth and seven other planets orbit (go around) the Sun, along with many smaller objects. Most of the planets have several moons orbiting them. Together, all these objects make up the Solar System. The word 'solar' means 'to do with the Sun'.

▶ Every object pulls on every other object. This is called gravity, and it holds you to the ground and keeps the planets orbiting the Sun. Gravity is weaker on planets that are less massive, which means that things weigh less. On Mars, you would weigh about one-third as much as on Earth.

Sun

Mercury

Venus

Earth

Mars

Jupiter

Superscience

Birth of the Solar System

The Solar System began as a dark cloud in space. Gravity pulled the cloud together, and it began to spin. Deep inside, it became thick, and so hot that it began to glow. This area turned into the Sun. Other parts of the cloud became the planets.

Nicholas Copernicus (1473–1543)

Centuries ago, most people believed the Sun and planets went round the Earth. Copernicus thought that the Earth and planets went round the Sun, but it was many years before people agreed with him.

Neptune

Uranus

Saturn

▶ Pluto is one of three known 'dwarf planets' – small, round worlds that orbit the Sun. There are thousands of even smaller worlds, called asteroids. Most of these orbit between Mars and Jupiter. Some have their own tiny moons.

CREATIVE CORNER

Walk through the Solar System

In a park, stick a flag in the ground. This is the Sun. Take three paces and stick in a flag for Mercury. Now put flags down after these distances:

3 paces (Venus)

2 (Earth)

4 (Mars)

28 (Jupiter)

34 (Saturn)

75 (Uranus)

84 (Neptune)

The Sun

Without the Sun there would be no life on Earth. Even the air would be frozen solid. As the Earth spins, the Sun shines on different areas. People living in those areas see the Sun rise in the east, move across the sky and set in the west.

▶ The Sun is a star, a vast ball of glowing gas, large enough to contain over one million planets the size of the Earth. Heat and light make their way outwards from the Sun's core. First they travel by radiation, and then by convection (see p.43).

Convective zone

Core

Radiative zone

Sun

◀ The Earth moves constantly around the Sun. The time it takes to complete one orbit is one year. This orbit is not quite circular, so the Earth is closest to the Sun in January and furthest away in July.

Earth's orbit

Earth

Sunspot

Prominence

? **WHY DOES THE SUN SHINE?**

The enormous gravity in the Sun's core squeezes atoms together until they merge into larger atoms. This releases vast amounts of energy from within the atoms.

▲ Explosions on the Sun throw fountains of hot gas high above its surface. These are called prominences. Sunspots are areas that are cooler than the rest of the Sun. Because of this coolness, they look darker.

CREATIVE CORNER

How to look at the Sun safely

Take two pieces of white cardboard and, using a sharp pencil, make a tiny hole in one. Standing with your back to the Sun, hold up the card with the hole and the other card about 20cm below it. Move the cards apart and together until the Sun's image is sharp. With luck, you may see some sunspots too.

X Never look directly at the Sun!

INTERNET LINKS: www.bbc.co.uk/science/space/solarsystem/sun_and_planets/sun

The Earth

The Earth, our world, is the third planet from the Sun. It turns constantly – in 24 hours it spins around once. It is daytime on the parts of the Earth that face the Sun.

▶ Life exists on Earth because there is air to breathe and water to drink. Earth's size gives it enough gravity, (pulling force) to hold on to the atmosphere, the layer of air that surrounds it. The Earth's distance from the Sun is right for water on the planet to be liquid.

Superscience

Inside the Earth

If you could look inside the Earth, you would see that the soil and oceans are a very thin layer on top of a rocky crust. Beneath this is a 'mantle' of different rocks. Under that is a layer of hot, liquid metal. The Earth's inner core is made of very hot, solid metal.

Mantle

Outer core

Inner core

Crust

The Earth's poles are covered in ice and snow.

This area is a hot, dry desert.

From space, much of the Earth is hidden by clouds.

The age of the Earth
The Earth is about 4,600 million years old, and the planet took millions of years to form. Earth was formed from dust in a great, dark cloud in space. The dust stuck together into lumps, which grew larger and attracted other lumps by the force of gravity.

Winter in the north
Summer in the south

Spring in the north
Autumn in the south

The Sun   North pole

Autumn in the north
Spring in the south

South pole

Summer in the north
Winter in the south

?

HOW MUCH OF THE EARTH IS COVERED IN WATER?
About 71 per cent of the Earth is covered in water. Most of this liquid is the salty water of the seas and oceans.

▲ Some parts of the Earth get a lot more heat and light from the Sun during some times of year than they do during others. We call these different times of year 'seasons'.

The Moon

The Moon is about 400,000 kilometres from Earth, and it is our planet's nearest neighbour in space. We see it glowing because the Sun shines on it.

▶ The Moon orbits the Earth about every 27 days. We only ever see one half of it from the Earth. The brighter parts are mountainous, and the darker areas, called seas, are flatter. The Moon is also marked with many bowl-shaped holes called craters.

Ocean of Storms

Copernicus Crater

Ptolemaeus Crater

Tycho Crater

Wernher von Braun (1912–1977)

The German scientist von Braun developed rockets used in World War II. He moved to the USA after the war and helped build rockets to explore outer space. He was in charge of building the Saturn V rocket that carried people to the Moon.

◀ The first astronauts (space-travellers) to reach the Moon arrived in 1969, on the US Apollo space-mission. There is no air on the Moon, so they had to wear space-suits. The astronauts weighed much less on the Moon than they did on Earth.

▶ A solar eclipse happens when the Moon passes exactly between the Sun and the Earth, and the Moon's shadow falls on parts of our planet. The Sun and sky become dark for people in those areas, although it is daytime.

Sea of Serenity

Sea of Tranquillity

Moon

Sun

Earth

Sea of Fertility

CREATIVE CORNER

The Man in the Moon

For thousands of years, people have imagined different shapes in the Moon. When the Moon is full, see if you can see any of these: a face, someone carrying sticks, a man and his dog, a rabbit, a crab, a girl reading. It is possible to see all sorts of things that are not really there! Keep a list and draw the things you see.

Rabbit

INTERNET LINKS: www.google.com/moon/ • http://eclipse.gsfc.nasa.gov/eclipse.html

▲ Mercury is the smallest planet and closest to the Sun. It has almost no atmosphere.

▲ Venus has a thick atmosphere and is the hottest planet. It is always cloudy there.

▲ Earth is home to many plants and animals. It has large oceans and icy poles.

▲ Mars has a thin atmosphere and icy poles. It is covered with reddish sand.

The planets

There are two kinds of planet in our Solar System. Mercury, Venus, Earth and Mars are small worlds of rock and metal. Jupiter, Saturn, Uranus and Neptune are all planets called gas giants. They have cold, deep atmospheres, rings of dust and rocks, and many moons.

VOCABULARY

atmosphere
Layers of gases around a planet or star.

poles
The 'ends' of a planet.

nitrogen
A substance that is a gas on Earth, but a solid or liquid on cold planets.

? IS THERE LIFE ON OTHER PLANETS?
Scientists have not yet found life on any other planets. However, it is possible that there may once have been life on Mars.

▲ Jupiter is the largest planet and has many moons. This is the view from one of them.

▲ Uranus was hit by an unknown planet-sized object long ago. Now it spins on its side.

▲ Neptune is the coldest and stormiest planet. There are nitrogen volcanoes on its largest moon.

▼ Saturn has large, bright rings. This is an imaginary view of the planet from Titan, Saturn's largest moon. Titan has lakes of thick, tar-like liquid and is the only moon in the Solar System with an atmosphere.

Johannes Kepler (1571–1630)
In Kepler's time, people thought the planets moved in perfect circles. Kepler discovered that they have oval orbits. He also found out that they move faster when they are closer to the Sun.

INTERNET LINKS: www.esa.int/esaKIDSen/Planetsandmoons.html

Space rubble

Our Solar System contains trillions of small chunks of rock and metal called meteoroids. In its cold outer regions, there are billions of lumps of mixed ice and rock. These are all leftovers from the birth of the Solar System, 4.6 billion years ago.

1. A boulder-sized meteorite falls to Earth.

2. The impact blasts rock into the air.

3. The blast forms a crater in the ground.

4. Over many years, the crater fills with soil.

▲ Meteoroids that fall to the Earth's surface are called meteorites. Very occasionally, they are so large that they form wide craters when they crash onto the ground.

WHERE DO COMETS COME FROM?

The outer part of the Solar System contains billions of icy rocks called cometary nuclei. Sometimes, these drift towards the Sun and turn into comets.

Edmond Halley (1656–1742)
Halley discovered that sometimes the same comets reappear in the sky. They do this because they move around the Sun in regular orbits. He worked out that one comet – now called Halley's comet – would return every 76 years.

◀ Comets are lumps of icy rock that travel on long journeys through space. When they get close to the Sun, they heat up. The ice changes to steam and a bright tail forms, which can sometimes be seen from Earth.

▶ When meteoroids fall through the Earth's atmosphere, they heat up and start to glow with light. These glows can be seen in the night sky as meteors, which are also called shooting stars.

CREATIVE CORNER

Spot a meteor

On a cloudless night, get as far as you can from bright lights, and look up at the sky. You may have to wait a while, so you could lie on your back on a sleeping bag. Meteors appear when the Earth passes through dusty areas of space.

X Only do this with an adult

INTERNET LINKS: www.bbc.co.uk/science/space/solarsystem/other_solar_system_bodies/asteroid

Stars and nebulae

The stars are enormous balls of glowing gas. Many are brighter than the Sun, but the Sun is very much closer to Earth, so it looks much brighter than any other star.

◀ ▼ The largest stars are called supergiants. Some are so large that millions of objects the size of the Sun could fit inside them. The Sun is a medium-sized star called a yellow dwarf. White dwarfs are much smaller than the Sun, and are the shrunken remains of dead stars.

Supergiant

Sun

White dwarf

Superscience

Supernovae and black holes

When the most massive stars run out of fuel, they destroy themselves in huge explosions called supernovae. The centre of the dead star remains as a tiny, crushed object called a black hole. The gravity of a black hole is so strong that even light cannot escape from it.

▲ Stars are often grouped into clusters. The Pleiades cluster is the easiest to see from Earth. Many of its stars are hotter and bluer than the Sun. The stars look hazy because they are inside a cloud of dust.

▲ A nebula is a patch of hazy light or darkness in the sky. The Orion nebula (above) is named after the constellation it is in. It is an area of dust and gas where new stars are being born.

HOW MANY STARS ARE THERE?
There are at least a thousand billion billion stars in the Universe – more than the number of grains of sand on all the beaches of the world.

► This is a part of the Orion nebula called the Horsehead. It is an area of dust and gas. We can see it only because it blocks the light from the glowing gas behind it.

INTERNET LINKS: www.kidscosmos.org/cosmos/cosmos_stars.php

Looking at the stars

On a clear, dark night, you can see around 2,000 stars. Using telescopes, astronomers (scientists who study the stars) can see millions more. They can work out how far away the stars are and what they are made of.

Orion

◄ For thousands of years people have made patterns (called constellations) out of the stars in the sky, and named them after people and animals. This is the constellation of Orion, who was a hunter in ancient Greek legends.

Superscience

Radio telescopes

Many objects in space give out invisible radio waves. Radio telescopes use huge dishes to collect these waves. Computers then make pictures and maps of the objects that sent out the waves. Sometimes, radio telescopes all over the world point to the same object, to gather as many radio waves as possible.

Primary mirror

Eyepiece lens

Secondary mirror

Light

Eyepiece lens

Objective lens

147

▲ Reflecting telescopes, or 'reflectors', use mirrors to gather light. The main mirror is called the primary and the smaller one is the secondary. The world's largest telescopes are all reflectors.

▼ You can see more with a telescope if you allow your eyes 15 minutes to get used to the darkness. Leaning your elbows on a wall will steady the image.

▲ Refracting telescopes use lenses (see p.37). The main lens is called the objective. Reflectors and refractors both use an eyepiece lens to send the light to the eye, or to a camera or other instrument.

CREATIVE CORNER

Make a simple telescope

At night, hold a small magnifying glass very close to one eye and hold a larger one at arm's length. Look through both towards a street light and move the larger one slowly towards you until the streetlight looks sharp. Try looking at stars or the Moon in this way. Some telescopes that astronomers use work like this, making stars look closer and brighter.

INTERNET LINKS: http://spaceplace.nasa.gov/starfinder/

Launch
escape
rocket

Command
module

Service
module

Lunar
module

Third
stage

Second
stage

First
stage

Space travellers

The first space traveller was a dog called Laika, which means 'barker' in Russian. She travelled in the Sputnik 2 spaceship in 1957. The first human space traveller was cosmonaut Yuri Gagarin, in 1961. Both Laika and Gagarin orbited the Earth.

◄ All space-travellers need rockets to launch them into space. This is the Saturn V Moon-rocket. To reduce its mass, its three stages were each left behind once the fuel they carried was used up.

VOCABULARY
astronaut
A space-traveller from America or any other English-speaking country.
cosmonaut
A space-traveller from Russia or the USSR.

◄ Space shuttles were used for travelling to space stations and satellites. They took off like rockets, but landed back on Earth just like planes. The 30-year-old shuttle programme ended in 2011.

CAN YOU FIND?

1. a helmet
2. a back-pack
3. a space-suit
4. a space shuttle
5. a rocket

▲ This astronaut has left his spaceship to carry out some repairs. This is called a space-walk. There is no air in space, so the astronaut has to wear a space-suit to protect himself.

CREATIVE CORNER

Make a balloon-powered rocket

Tie a string about 2m long to the back of a chair. Thread a straw onto it and attach two pieces of sticky tape to the straw. Tie the other end of the string to another chair. Blow up the balloon and stick it to the tape. Now let go! Rockets work like this – gases rush out of them and push them along.

INTERNET LINKS: www.nasa.gov/mission_pages/shuttle/main/index.html

Machines in orbit

There are thousands of machines called satellites orbiting the Earth. Some are used for forecasting the weather, spying or mapping. Others receive and transmit TV or phone signals. Satellites with people on board are called space stations.

◀ The first satellite was called Sputnik, and it orbited the Earth in 1957. It was launched by the USSR (Union of Soviet Socialist Republics). During each orbit, which took about 96 minutes, it sent out signals that could be heard on radios throughout the world.

Superscience

Microgravity

On board a space station, people and objects weigh almost nothing. They float around if they are not fixed down. The tiny weights that objects still have are caused by, among other things, the gravity produced by the space station itself. This is called microgravity.

▲ Skylab was a US space station that went into orbit in 1973. It was used to study the Sun and the effects of microgravity. It crashed back to Earth in 1979.

Zvezda module
(living quarters)

Robot
arm

Columbus laboratory

? HOW HIGH IS A SATELLITE?

Satellites orbit at least 160km above the Earth. Closer to the ground, the air is thick enough to slow them down and make them crash.

▲ The International Space Station has had people on board since 2000. It is being built by the scientists of 16 countries, and will be the size of a football pitch when it is complete. It is powered by sunlight and is used for scientific research.

Solar panel, to
make electricity
from sunlight

► The higher you go above the Earth, the less air there is. This means that stars and planets can be seen more clearly. The Hubble Space Telescope has been in orbit at a height of around 300 kilometres since 1990 and has sent amazing images of the Universe back to Earth.

INTERNET LINKS: www.nasa.gov/mission_pages/station/main/index.html

Space robots

Space probes are robot spaceships without crews, sent to explore the Universe. Simple ones fly past planets, taking photographs as they pass. More complicated ones deliver orbiters, landers or rovers to explore the worlds they visit.

Superscience

Star probes

Five probes that were originally sent to explore other planets are now on long journeys to the stars. They will not arrive for thousands of years. They are carrying messages for any aliens that might find them.

◄ The Cassini-Huygens probe reached Saturn in 2004. The Cassini orbiter studied Saturn from space, while the Huygens lander was sent to Titan, Saturn's largest moon. Titan has an atmosphere, so a parachute was used for a safe landing.

? WHEN WAS THE FIRST SPACE PROBE LAUNCHED?
The first space probe was the Russian Luna 1, which flew by the Moon in 1959. It is still in orbit around the Sun.

▲ The Phoenix lander reached Mars in 2008. It had a robotic arm to scoop up the soil and search for signs of life. Phoenix's mission ended in 2010.

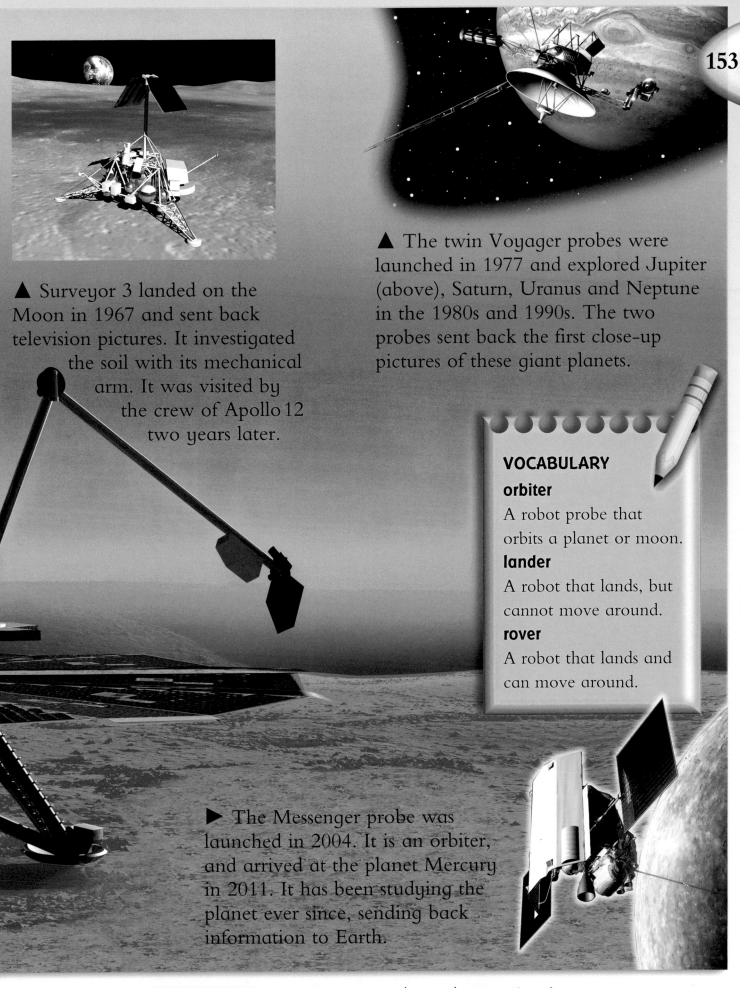

▲ Surveyor 3 landed on the Moon in 1967 and sent back television pictures. It investigated the soil with its mechanical arm. It was visited by the crew of Apollo 12 two years later.

▲ The twin Voyager probes were launched in 1977 and explored Jupiter (above), Saturn, Uranus and Neptune in the 1980s and 1990s. The two probes sent back the first close-up pictures of these giant planets.

VOCABULARY

orbiter
A robot probe that orbits a planet or moon.

lander
A robot that lands, but cannot move around.

rover
A robot that lands and can move around.

▶ The Messenger probe was launched in 2004. It is an orbiter, and arrived at the planet Mercury in 2011. It has been studying the planet ever since, sending back information to Earth.

Now you know!

▲ The Universe began in a 'Big Bang' about 13,700 million years ago. It has been growing ever since.

▶ Robot spaceships from Earth have visited all the planets in our Solar System. Some are now on their way to the stars.

▶ The Earth is one of eight planets that orbit the Sun. The Sun and planets, together with moons, dust, comets and rubble, form the Solar System.

▲ Stars are grouped together into galaxies. Our galaxy is called the Milky Way.

◀ No life has been found anywhere except on Earth, but it may once have existed on Mars.

◀ There are billions and billions of stars, and the Sun is one of them. Some stars are much larger than the Sun, while others are smaller.

▲ People landed on the Moon in 1969. So far, people have not travelled further into space than the Moon.

Facts and figures

Here is some extra information for you to explore.

Simple shapes

Flat shapes

Circle	**Triangle**	**Square**	**Pentagon**	**Hexagon**
1 edge	3 edges	4 edges	5 edges	6 edges
0 corners	3 corners	4 corners	5 corners	6 corners

Solid shapes

Sphere	**Cylinder**	**Tetrahedron**	**Pyramid**	**Cube**
1 surface	3 surfaces	4 surfaces	5 surfaces	6 surfaces
0 edges	2 edges	6 edges	8 edges	12 edges
0 corners	0 corners	4 corners	5 corners	8 corners

Some important scientific laws

Law of gravity
Every object pulls on every other object with the force of gravity. The pull is stronger the more massive the objects are, and the closer they are together.

First law of motion
A moving object will keep moving at the same speed in the same direction unless something forces it to change its speed or direction.

Conservation of Energy (First Law of Thermodynamics)
Energy cannot appear or disappear, it can only change into a different sort of energy.

Second Law of Thermodynamics
Heat always moves from hotter things (or places) to cooler ones.

Magnetic poles
The north pole of a magnet pushes away other north poles and pulls south poles.
The south pole of a magnet pushes away other south poles and pulls north poles.

Some important elements

Carbon is the element on which all living things are based.
Gold is a soft shiny metal that is expensive and quite rare.
Hydrogen is the lightest element and the commonest in the Universe
Iron is a metal, often used to make steel; the Earth is made mostly of iron.
Nitrogen is the commonest gas in the air.
Oxygen is the gas in air that we need to breathe.
Silicon is found in rock and used to make glass, cement and many other things.
Uranium is a metal that is used as fuel in nuclear power stations.

The history of life on Earth

4.54 billion years ago: Earth forms
about 3.8 billion years ago: life begins in the oceans
about 530 million years ago: the first fish evolve
about 500 million years ago: first land plants and land animals
about 400 million years ago: first amphibians
about 310 million years ago: first reptiles
about 230 million years ago: first dinosaurs
about 210 million years ago: first mammals
about 150 million years ago: first birds
65 million years ago: most dinosaurs die out
190 thousand years ago: modern humans evolve

The planets of the Solar System

Planet	Average distance from Sun, compared to Earth	Average diameter, compared to Earth	Mass, compared to Earth	Length of day	Length of year
Mercury	0.39	0.38	0.06	176 Earth days	88 Earth days
Venus	0.72	0.95	0.82	117 Earth days	225 Earth days
Earth	1	1	1	24 hours	365.24 days
Mars	1.5	0.53	0.11	24 hours 37 mins	687 Earth days
Jupiter	5.2	10.9	318	9 hours 55 mins	12 Earth years
Saturn	9.6	9.0	95	10 hours 39 mins	29.5 Earth years
Uranus	19.2	19.2	15	17 hours 14 mins	84 Earth years
Neptune	30.1	3.9	17	16 hours 7 mins	265 Earth years

(On average, the Earth is 150 million kilometres from the Sun and has
a diameter of 12,742 km. Its mass is 6 trillion trillion kilogrammes.)

Index

Acknowledgements

The publisher would like to thank Deborah Bloxham and Dan Albert at the Science Museum.

The publisher would also like to thank the following illustrators:
Mike Atkinson, Julian Baker, Julian Baum, Mark Bergin, Peter Bull, Peter Dennis (Linda Rogers), Richard Draper, Michael Fisher, Chris Forsey, Terry Gabbey, Adam Hook (Linden Artists), Christian Hook, Tony Kenyon, Mike Lacey, Stuart Lafford (Linden Artists), Stephen Lings (Linden Artists), Chris Lyon, Patricia Ludlow, Kevin Maddison, Shane Marsh (Linden Artists), Damir Martin, Steve Noon, Chris Orr, Nicki Palin, Sebastian Quigley (Linden Artists), Mike Saunders, Rob Shone, Clive Spong, Treve Tamblin, Chris Turnball, Roger Ward, Steve Weston (Linden Artists), David Wright

All Creative Corner illustrations by Jo Moore

Every effort has been made to credit the artists whose work appears in this book. The publishers would like to apologize for any inadvertent omissions. We will be pleased to amend the acknowledgements in any future editions.